ESSENTIALS OF VISUAL INTERPRETATION

D09999204

"This slim but substantial volume is a joy to read and strikes a good balance between rigor and accessibility."
—*Dolores Flamiano, James Madison University, USA*

Essentials of Visual Interpretation explains how to talk and write critically about visual media and to examine how evolving visual environments, media, and technologies affect human self-understanding and culture formation.

Lively and accessibly written chapters provide a solid foundation in the tools and ideas of visual meaning, familiarizing readers with a growing, cross-cultural subfield, and preparing them to pursue thoughtful work in a variety of related disciplines. The authors include rich examples and illustrations—ranging from cave paintings to memes, from optical science to visual analytics, from ancient pictographs to smart phones—that engage students with the fascinating complexity of visual interpretation. Each chapter introduces students to key terms and concepts relevant to visual analysis, with ideas for short individual or group exercises to enhance understanding.

The book is ideal as a primer in visual analysis and visual communication for students in courses within communication studies, cultural studies, digital humanities, semiotics, media studies, and visual anthropology.

Online support materials include multimedia activities for students and links to additional resources for students and instructors.

Rachel R. Reynolds is Associate Professor of Communication and Graduate Faculty in Communication, Culture & Media at Drexel University in Philadelphia. She researches discourse and semiotics of race, immigration, and gender.

Greg Niedt is an Instructor in the Liberal Arts department at the Pennsylvania Academy of the Fine Arts (PAFA) in Philadelphia. Greg's research focuses on how discourses of cultural, gender, and linguistic diversity are represented in the urban landscape.

ESSENTIALS OF VISUAL INTERPRETATION

Rachel R. Reynolds
Greg Niedt

NEW YORK AND LONDON

First published 2021
by Routledge
52 Vanderbilt Avenue, New York, NY 10017

and by Routledge
2 Park Square, Milton Park, Abingdon, Oxon, OX14 4RN

Routledge is an imprint of the Taylor & Francis Group, an informa business

Library of Congress Cataloging-in-Publication Data

Names: Reynolds, Rachel R., author. | Niedt, Greg, author.
Title: Essentials of visual interpretation / Rachel R. Reynolds, Greg Niedt.
Description: New York, NY : Routledge, 2021. | Includes bibliographical
   references and index.
Identifiers: LCCN 2020038042 (print) | LCCN 2020038043 (ebook) |
   ISBN 9780367491284 (paperback) | ISBN 9780367492403 (hardback) |
   ISBN 9781003045274 (ebook)
Subjects: LCSH: Visual communication.
Classification: LCC P93.5 .R489 2021 (print) | LCC P93.5 (ebook) |
   DDC 302.2/26—dc23
LC record available at https://lccn.loc.gov/2020038042
LC ebook record available at https://lccn.loc.gov/2020038043

ISBN: 978-0-367-49128-4 (pbk)
ISBN: 978-0-367-49240-3 (hbk)
ISBN: 978-1-003-04527-4 (ebk)

Typeset in Bembo
by KnowledgeWorks Global Ltd.

Visit the eResource at https://www.routledge.com/9780367491284.

CONTENTS

IMAGES

IMAGE ACKNOWLEDGMENTS AND ATTRIBUTIONS

The author and publishers would like to thank or acknowledge the following artists and organizations.

Chapter One

1.1 Photographer Unknown, U.S. Library of Congress, National Red Cross Collection
1.2 Lewis Hine, U.S. Library of Congress, National Child Labor Committee Collection
1.3 Haryadi CH, Shutterstock
1.4 Reynolds and Niedt

Chapter Two

2.1 Drawing courtesy of Steve McCall
2.2 Reproduced with permission from Thomson, G. and Macpherson, F. (July 2017), "Kanizsa's Triangles" in F. Macpherson (ed.), *The Illusions Index*. Retrieved from https://www.illusionsindex.org/i/kanizsa-triangle
2.3 Copyright © Lemel Yossi for Amnesty International Israel

Chapter Five

5.1 Mihai Popa – Travel, Alamy Stock Photo
5.2 Slawomir Kowalewski, Shutterstock
5.3 Photo courtesy of Greg Niedt

Chapter Six

6.1 Knowyourmeme.com
6.2 Original Photo by Dave Roth. With permission of Dave and Zoe Roth

Chapter Seven

7.1 National Archive of the Netherlands
7.2 Chronicle, Alamy Stock Photo

Chapter Eight

8.1 Monkey Business, Shutterstock
8.2 Lazy Llama, Shutterstock

Chapter Nine

9.1 Uun Tsani, Wikimedia Commons
9.2 Photo courtesy of Greg Niedt
9.3 Crew of Apollo 17, NASA

AUTHORS' ACKNOWLEDGMENTS

When we told students, colleagues, friends, and family that we wanted to create a guidebook to understanding how images work in contemporary life, their responses were overwhelmingly, "I need to read a book like that." Despite the growth in images as a primary means of communication in mass media and social media, many people find it hard to create a dialog that moves from image to word in order to express their feelings and experiences with the visuality that saturates contemporary life. We hope that this book in its breadth as well as its periodic close-ups on phenomena like memes, multimodality, cognition and vision, and other sections, will help people to develop a useful and fun visual and verbal repertoire to explore meaning making through image.

Reynolds would like to especially thank Kristina Dziedzic-Wright, Beth Anne Buggenhagen, Todd Starkweather, Sara Beth Keough, Daniel Freed, Patti Renda, Charles Morscheck, Michael Lee, Steve McCall, and Ben Page for their help with various portions of the text. She is also very grateful to Maria Giovanna Musso and Flavia Orlandi at SAPIENZA, University of Rome, as well as dear friend Marcantonio Graffeo for their support while she drafted portions of the manuscript.

Niedt would like to thank Mathilde Dissing Christensen for sharing long, supportive hours at the café while the ideas for this book were first coming together, Julia Hildebrand and Julia C. Richmond for their insights and suggestions, and Tavia Nyong'o for his spiritual encouragement. Shout-out also to the undergraduate Visual Anthropology class, Fall 2018, whose feedback on the pilot versions of some of these chapters was instrumental to the development of the text.

And we would both like to thank Afrooz Mossallaeipour, Katarzyna Elliot-Maksymovicz, Nick Coffman and Wesley Shumar at Drexel University for their help oiling the gears of this project. Alex Jenkins was also instrumental in enhancing the materials on video gaming in Chapter 8 and we thank him heartily. And thank you to the four anonymous reviewers who read and commented on this manuscript, for the valuable and practical advice.

1

HOW IS SEEING A CULTURAL PRACTICE?

Introduction

There's an old saying that goes, "We see things not as they are, but as we are." Among the many other idioms and metaphors that rely on sight to make their point (in English: "seeing is believing," "I couldn't believe my eyes," etc.), this is one of the few that calls attention to how subjective sight can be. Those of us who can see often think of sight as the most reliable of the senses, whose evidence can be trusted, yet we often forget that what we see is subject to biology, culture, and experience. So much of what we see—comprehension, interpretation, reaction—unfolds differently for every person. Our purpose with this book is to take apart that process, and encourage you, the reader, to think more deeply about what it means for you to see the world. How might your perception and ability to "read" the meanings in the world you see around you (hence, *visual interpretation*) be different than someone else's? This chapter is intended to start you on the path to understanding how much more complicated seeing is than you might realize.

It makes sense to begin a discussion of visual meaning with an image or two. You are probably not familiar with either of the two images below even though they have special place in American and world visual history. Take a close look at both of them now (Images 1.1. and 1.2), without captions.

First, we should distinguish *vision*, the biological mechanism of sight, from *visuality*, how we interpret the data we receive from sight. The two are intertwined, but nobody's vision is perfect enough by itself to give them all the data they need, and visuality's interpretations always incorporate some pre-existing ideas about the world. Still, there are some commonalities to what we perceive in the world and how we perceive it. For instance, what is your eye drawn to first in these photos? Chances are it will be the subjects' faces; humans, like all primates, are hardwired to recognize the elements that comprise

IMAGE 1.1

IMAGE 1.2

faces and facial expressions too. Consider the ways the boys' heads are slightly tilted and the slight curvature of the lips on the face of the boy on the right. What emotion would you say he is experiencing in this photo? What about how both boys are holding objects in one hand and apparently manipulating those objects with the other? Even if you didn't know the title of the image, you might guess that the boys are playing, or working with some sort of purpose or direction (the paint can in the foreground could also be a tip off). At the instinctual level, you can make immediate assumptions about what you're seeing because your brain is a superb organizer of information, most of all with information about other humans. The immediate visual information you receive combines with your memory and cognition to play a key role in your initial impressions of the world around you, the other people moving through it, and representations of them in media.

This is one kind of literate interpretation of visual material: reading the face to determine a person's emotional state, or reading basic clues about what they are doing (or intend to do). What about reading the wider context of the photo? The style of the clothes and hair, the skin and features of the subject, the style of the models and the wooden box the boys are working with, and the barely noticeable woman in a cloth cap in the background, all might give you important hints. But the *medium* itself, a black-and-white photograph, is also a clue. (Medium is the object, virtual or real, through which the art or other message is created and presented—charcoal and paper; pixels and Photoshop; acrylic on canvas; ink on paper). Given the length of time humans have been creating visual representations, photography is a relatively recent technology. Depending on your knowledge of its history, you can probably make a reasonable guess about when this picture was taken, especially if you draw on other contextual elements in the scene.

When we add some descriptive context, your interpretive abilities will perhaps greatly increase. If you are told that the photo was taken in the United States during the influenza pandemic in 1919, how does this bit of historical knowledge alter your idea of the boys' situation and their activity? And how might your idea of them differ from someone else's? After all, there is nothing about the photo's contents that would indicate disease or another public crisis. As you start to consider how your impressions of the same shapes, colors, and patterns of light differ from other people's, you start to move from just vision to visuality. Through history and across cultures, the former has changed very little, but the latter is highly variable.

Now take a look at the girls in Image 1.2, which you might guess comes from the same era as the boys in Image 1.1. But Image 1.2 is much different in setting, subjects' pose and clothing, and the nature of the background observer, a much younger boy, who is silently watching the girls as they are photographed. What are these subjects thinking and what can you tell about their day in this scene? They are dressed in coats and hats, and have their hands firmly in pocket—it looks to be cold out. What if you hear that the title of this photograph is *Newsgirls Waiting for Papers*? The evolution of media (and indeed, child labor laws) has dramatically affected the role of the newspaper in daily life, at least in the United States, to the point that newspapers no longer rely upon youths to sell them on the streets or to deliver them anymore. Even with different clothes and a full-color image, could you envision a photo with this title being made in the present day?

Not all images will be equally easy to read across all the dimensions of visuality. Scenes like the one in Image 1.1 might emphasize the work, leisure, or school environment of the two boys rather than close-up portrayal of the boys themselves. It is in fact titled, *Back Yard Workshop*, a title that will probably further trigger your interpretation of both what the boys are up to, as well as the intent of the photographer in sharing their activity with the viewer. Meanwhile, the formal portrait-like quality of *Newsgirls* is rather different and might make you ask what was the purpose of the photographer in highlighting the individuals rather than their activities?

But however rich or sparse the streams of information are, you will rely on your previous experiences to further frame the details of the image. For example, the presence of the word *workshop* in the title of Image 1.1 carries a great deal of weight, while it's already pretty easy to guess that they are in a back yard. Once you are able to pair the image with that word, you begin to apply all your knowledge and ideologies of what *work* is, as well as the concept of childhood and perhaps schooling under quarantine, given the photo's pandemic context. Remember that once you move past your basic visual instincts, it is impossible to examine a photo like this without any of your pre-existing prejudice or cultural judgments shaping your opinion. People who have been homeschooled in the COVID-19 epidemic will emotionally and intellectually, indeed experientially, see the photo differently than those who haven't. Likewise, those who have grown up in the smartphone, video-on-demand, and online schooling era, or those who associate schooling with college readiness, rather than vocational education, might find the idea of a backyard-based schooling activity unusual or quaintly old-fashioned. The fact that the boys are white adolescents will also have different weight to different viewers. This variability in seeing lies at the core of visuality; acknowledging that each of us has a unique personal and social history of experience (or *subjectivity*) helps us understand why a single, fixed image can have so many different intentions and interpretations.

Nevertheless, certain habits and inclinations in interpretation—of portraits for example—can gain a kind of density over time, becoming culturally fixed as a benchmark against which all others are measured. That can be said of the personality and connection that comes through to us in the desire of the two photographers (they were different people) to create strong photographic portraits of their subjects. With both the reading of the photos and their creation, we can talk about their *aesthetics*, the philosophical idea of what makes something art, or at least artistic. Look at how the photographers have composed or selected elements of the scenes here. How do they compare to other historical or documentary photographs you've seen, especially those from the early 20th century, or those of young people? What "rules" must a photographer consider that, say, a political cartoonist or fashion photographer wouldn't have to?

Once we begin to move even further outside the frames and captions of the photos themselves—literally and figuratively— we can start trying to read their purposes and effects at another level. Would you have a different opinion of these photos if you saw them hanging a museum, instead of in this book? What about if they were part of an exhibition or website created to illustrate the story of the American Red Cross? Or what if they were created as a political project to document the widespread nature of child labor exploitation in the United States, one that successfully spurred legislators into creating new labor laws and schooling opportunities for children and youth? Both photos are part of named digital collections of historical significance in the United States Library of Congress. Image 1.1 or *Back Yard Workshop* is part of a collection of over 50,000 photos with negatives that were donated to the Library of Congress in 1944 and 1952 with the understanding that they belonged to the American people.

The collection captures a specific time span and purpose in the history of photographic documentation. Since the beginning of the 20th century, the American Red Cross had sent professional photographers as part of their Magazine Bureau to document their humanitarian work in war zones, disaster areas, and with the poor and the sick. Although Image 1.1 could perhaps also be considered an early version of a nonprofit promotional photo, it reflects the richness of historical events like the influenza pandemic—in this case, in Denver, Colorado, for the National American Red Cross Mountain Division. Fortunately, in a collection that wasn't fully indexed, or for which at least some documentation data has been lost, more data on a card associated with the image tells us that it was taken "while School was closed for Influenza." Now that we know this, we may begin to appreciate that the woman on the steps is more than likely a Red Cross worker or full-time volunteer (and rather than forgotten, honored today through this collection), wearing a very nurse-like uniform that includes a full head covering. Likewise, we may start to notice that the boy on the left is in short pants and that his shirt is outsized for his still childlike frame. We may conclude that the boys are either temporarily or permanently without family; at the very least, there is some mystery surrounding why they were left to the Red Cross for guidance and care during the Pandemic. Read a little further on that card, however, and it references the Junior Red Cross, so one starts to wonder if these boys are themselves volunteers, helping out by making toys for younger children.

By contrast, the photo of the *Newsgirls* was taken by well-known child labor activist Lewis Hine in Hartford, Connecticut in 1908. Hine was a sociologist and a teacher, not a trained photographer; this particular portrait photo is one of his better artistic efforts. Typical of the notes Hine and his helpers wrote on photo prints, the back of this one reads: "Largest girl, Alice Goldman has been selling for 4 years. News dealer says she uses viler language than the newsboys do. Bessie Goldman and Bessie Brownstein are 9 years old and have been selling about one year. All sell until 7 or 7:30 P.M. daily. Location: Hartford, Connecticut."

These words give us a lot more about how *Newsgirls Waiting for Papers* works as a cultural and historical object. Unlike the first photo, we have names and even personalities of the subjects, something exceedingly rare in photos from this era. We see some of the evidence of how Hine worked. He had quit his job to spend two dozen years criss-crossing the country, collecting photos with names, stories, circumstances, and, crucially, the ages of very young people who were working 10–16 hour days, 7 days a week. This effort was a form of relatively new socially active investigative journalism called "muckraking," in which practices of exploitation and corruption were unearthed and documented in order to effect social change. In his trips, Hine generated thousands of photographs, demonstrating the human and economic toll of child labor on the people of the United States to both politicians and the public. His mission is reflected a bit today in the title of the Library of Congress Collection in which his photos are stored: The National Child Labor Committee Collection. At first glance, the photo that seemed like just another antique artifact has become a touchpoint for exploring the period it depicts in a deep and complex way.

These photos above require different kinds of work from you as a reader, starting with the initial look that leads you to draw some tentative conclusions about the subjects. Captions and other immediate elements are also part of what forms your understanding, an example of combining information from different elements like words and the photos together called multimodality, which we will refer to frequently in this book. And you draw on your general knowledge of cultural contexts, including everyday practices and logics that are almost unspoken to start to figure out what is going on as well. Finally, you integrate what you think you've "seen" as objective knowledge into wider contexts that tell you about history and beliefs, and how those might connect to the intent of the photo, or why it was made in the first place. Throughout this book, we will examine these processes in many situations and forms. The goal is to enhance your overt sense of *what "seeing" is*, and how to talk about it.

Note that many important terms are italicized and bolded in spots where they are first defined, and then elaborated. They also appear in an index at the end of the book so that you can easily look them up, and hopefully become comfortable with using them. Likewise, exercises at the end of each chapter are geared toward applying the abstract ideas we've introduced to interpreting visual elements of other unique images and situations, exploring how visual culture is created and responded to in daily life. Finally, we give a few suggestions for more in-depth exploration of chapter topics, for those of you interested in learning more.

CULTURE

We mostly use the word "culture" here in a way that echoes anthropologist E.B. Tylor's definition: "that complex whole which includes knowledge, belief, art, morals, law, custom, and any other capabilities and habits acquired by man as a member of society." Most anthropologists think of culture as a blueprint for our beliefs and behaviors, something acquired rather than consciously learned. We participate in multiple cultures throughout our lives, from broad national cultures to small-scale cultures of schools, workplaces, etc. But be careful—many people also define culture as *high culture*, meaning the arts, literature, and other humanistic achievements. We will address these too, as visual culture often involves both definitions in relation to our collective ways of seeing and interpreting the world.

Cultural practices, including visual ones, often feel natural to the people raised in them. Yet, practices will differ significantly between two places or times. Think of the variations in comics and animation between United States and Japanese culture, or how the practices of using maps and giving directions have changed since the introduction of smartphones. Which visual practices are you most comfortable with? How many visual cultures are you part of? (The answer is probably "more than you think.")

Key Terms in Visual Literacy

In order to understand contemporary visuality and how it informs our analysis of visual pieces like *Back Yard Workshop* and *Newsgirls Waiting for Papers*, among many others, there are two key terms that we will continually refer back to: multimodality and semiosis. Our ways of seeing are culturally bounded and highly variable, but these two terms describe processes that underlie the creation and interpretation of all visual media, regardless of when and where they are made.

Multimodality

The concept of *multimodality* was developed primarily by theorist Gunther Kress to help us map out how many different modes of communication—the visual, the linguistic, the sensory, and others—come together to make meaning that is greater than the sum of their parts. For Kress, interpretations of meaning are affected simultaneously by visual, linguistic, and cognitive processes, and each new attempt at meaning-making is affected by prior experience. Thus, our ability to "read" various modes, individually and in tandem, is part of the lifelong practice of interpreting everything in our environment. Moreover, each mode, be it photographic image, drawing, writing, fonts, graphics, etc., has its own special qualities that we take into account when we interpret what we see.

One way to consider the implications of multimodality is through Marshall McLuhan's famous edict, "the medium is the message." Why did Lewis Hine document thousands of children through photographs rather than articles in order to portray their exploitation as workers directly to the viewer? And why did the American Red Cross create a Magazine Bureau that featured professionally made photographs? To borrow another old adage, "a picture is worth a thousand words"—photos are interpreted and absorbed as evidence or truths in powerful and particular ways that another medium, such as text by itself, may not generate. Multimodality acknowledges that *not all ways of meaning-making are created equal*; to some extent, this is what makes the combination of media forms so potent. Kress also discusses how the process of interpreting and absorbing images affects our orientation toward knowledge systems and political beliefs. In particular, he says that each moment we interpret an image and its context is an ideologically laden moment, where the efforts to make meaning involve choices about belief and truth that are often political. As with *Newsgirls Waiting for Papers*, or *Back Yard Workshop*, attempts to interpret the images will result in some sort of political and emotional appeal, ranging from (for example) empathy with these three young girls and small boy standing in the cold, to concern over the social welfare of children and families torn apart and missing schooling in a deadly epidemic (or perhaps a sense of wellness and relief that these two boys are cared for by the American Red Cross in a frightening time).

Multimodality is also about examining how all the various layers or elements of meaning-making interact. The fact that these two images above are at the beginning of the first chapter, and that we have labeled them as "Images 1.1 and 1.2," gives you a heads-up that they will be an important focal point for grasping the main ideas of this book. We omitted captions as well, only revealing them later as an aid to interpretation. Doing this illustrates how placement and caption are both elements of the multimodal whole, as is the physicality of your experience while viewing it. (Are you reading this on paper in a book held in your hands, on an e-reader, or in a pirated PDF?) That the photos are in black and white and that the photographers were not credited directly in the caption also affects your interpretation. In fact, Lewis Hine's full notes on *Newsgirls* would have most certainly tipped the balance of your interpretation away from the educative process of learning about visual literacy for which we initially presented the image. In other words, the case of your earliest experience with the photo in this chapter, photographic technology, and attribution to the artist are all *modalities*, channels of information that come together to make meaning in particular ways.

In sum, multimodality means taking every element of potential meaning-making into consideration when trying to grasp interpretation—visual, oral, auditory, linguistic signs, structures, and composition, as well as the technologies of production and reproduction, and the placement and circulation of images. Each item individually and in tandem has the potential to deeply affect each interpretation of the image by each individual viewer or "reader" of the image or the environment. We explore this more thoroughly in Chapter 5, but it is a concept that will remain relevant throughout the book.

Semiosis

We draw the term *semiosis* from the field of semiotics, which stems from the idea that linguistic *signs*, including each recognizable word we encounter, have some kind of meaning. At the core, meaning is based mainly on prior experience with similar meaningful sounds or shapes on the page because of something called **arbitrariness**: the ideas we link to a given word are (with a few exceptions) based on how the culture has trained us to interpret it, rather than something inherent to the word itself. A classic example is the word *cat* which any English speaker will recognize, when it is spoken or written, as a type of carnivore, usually domestic, and quite popular on the internet. But a speaker of Cherokee would recognize *eesa* as the sound symbol or Cherokee sign for cat, and in Finland, the word or sign for cat is *kissa*. Shared cultural convention, usually learned in infancy and early childhood, is how we are socialized into recognizing sound meanings, but they are arbitrary, and there is no inherent "cattyness" to any given word for cat. (On the other hand, the word for the sound it makes is surprisingly close to *meow* in lots of languages.)

Semiosis itself is really a fancy word for meaning-making, but ideas and approaches to understanding signs are very useful for pulling apart the actual mechanics of meaning making. Thus, semiosis refers to the process by which we create, recognize, interpret, or otherwise deal with signs. Importantly, the field has grown beyond the language examples above to include the realm of the visual, the aural, the olfactory, and so forth. Moreover, a sign doesn't have to be merely a physical, public-facing text, but a thing that *communicates meaning beyond itself to someone*. Part of the project of visual analysis is to understand how and why a sign can communicate what it does, and to whom. We can further break down the concept of a sign into the **signifier** and the **signified**, terms adopted from linguist Ferdinand de Saussure. Following the example above, *cat* would be a signifier, and the signified object it points to would be a fuzzy feline with (hopefully) four legs. There are other theories of sign structure, but for our purposes it will suffice to say that a sign consists of something that you see, hear, or otherwise sense, and a piece of information that you are meant to obtain thanks to that encounter. Broadly defined, a sign could be a word you hear that indicates some object in the world; it could be a drawing of a cigarette with a slash through it to indicate you should not smoke; or it could be police lights flashing behind you to get you to pull over to the side of the road.

There is another layer of arbitrariness to signs: the degree of difference between the signifier and the object to which it refers, versus the *class* of objects to which it refers. If someone says "cat" and there is no cat in the room, you are likely to imagine another cat than the one they have in mind. And yet, we all share a *general* idea of what the word "cat" means; this is very important as the basis for shared mental representations, which are necessary for communication. To further this referential principle, here is another famous example: if someone says, "That's George Washington," how likely is it that person is referring to the "real" George Washington? In general, "That's George Washington" actually refers to an image or idea or set of shared symbolic beliefs that people associate with George Washington. They're probably not directly referring to the *original* referent because the man himself is long dead, unless you're standing next to his grave, or are at some kind of historical reenactment. The relationships between signifiers and specific signifieds differ from those of signifiers and general signifieds, but because we sometimes use the same words and communication strategies for both, we have to deal with ambiguity, misinterpretations, and clarifications.

Arbitrariness must be dealt with by cultural convention, because without it, we would have no way to use all the arbitrary sounds of language to create a system of communication. The same thing is true for visual information; most of us grow up into a visual environment where we use shared convention to interpret visual signs in more or less the same way. Take, for example, the items in Image 1.3. Some need no explanation: you probably recognize the skull and crossbones,

IMAGE 1.3 Symbols—more and less iconic

a symbol originally found on medieval European grave markers that gradually came to indicate both pirate-infested waters of the 17th century, and today, poisonous substances. More abstract but equally familiar is the radiation hazard sign, which dates to the 1940s. These two symbols are highly conventionalized in that they are circulated widely and in specific ways, so that (hopefully) all viewers of them will recognize that they signify *danger*. But the other symbols illustrate how less conventionalized images are just harder to interpret, and for any of them we don't encounter frequently—if ever—their meanings might be completely opaque, and certainly arbitrary, to us.

Iconicity, within the field of semiotics, refers to how much a signifier directly resembles or in some way imitates its referent. (This is different from when the words "icon" and "iconic" are used to refer to celebrities and the like.) Iconic visual signs, such as the wine glass in the first row that signifies *fragile*, are a little less arbitrary than purely symbolic things like the radiation hazard sign, which is entirely established by convention. (This doesn't mean that its creation was random; hazard signs are often vaguely triangular like this, so that they are quickly recognizable no matter which way the package is turned.) You can recognize a wine glass in silhouette, noticing a tear or fracture coming apart when you study the sign, and get some sense of the meaning. This does, however, require that you've had experience with wine glasses and substances that crack like glass in order to correctly interpret the intended iconic qualities of the sign. Nonetheless, the image matches on some level, or resembles what you imagine a wine glass to be.

There are other signs here which are iconic, but ambiguous enough that they require more formal knowledge of packaging labels to understand. Take the fifth symbol in the first row, for example: a square above two crooked shapes. You can probably recognize that they are meant to represent hands, but what is the intention here? Or, going to the second-to-last row, there's a pentagon with "Ex" inside it. Presumably, this is an abbreviation for a word that starts with "Ex," but which one out of the dozens, even hundreds, of possibilities? And why the pentagon? There may be other signs here which you have never seen before, but that are sufficiently iconic that you can perhaps deduce their meaning. All of this reminds us that humans regularly create signs to attend to our business of creating and transmitting culture, even the practices as seemingly mundane as making packaging labels, and thus semiotics lies at the foundation of interpreting many aspects of human communication.

PLANNED ICONICITY

While some signs accrue their meanings over time, there are also bodies that regulate them. The ISO (International Organization for Standardization) established many of the symbols in Image 1.3 for universal labeling standards, and governments often determine the form and use of road signs. This raises another question: who has the "right" to use signs to communicate their meanings? Or to repurpose them to create new meanings (like a stop sign on a bedroom door)? Scollon and Scollon (2003) point out that these discourses in place can open whole new levels of understanding iconicity.

Obviously, there are advantages to standardizing symbols worldwide; it makes sense for "danger" to mean "danger" everywhere. But it's very difficult to create a truly global visual culture without one group's practices taking precedence. For example, colors are often attributed meaning. In the United States, red can imply danger or passion, while in China, red can suggest good luck, and in India, red is a color for weddings. With these differences between cultural ideas of what visual information means in the world, people who create iconicity for global purposes have to be careful not to prioritize one culture's ways of seeing over another's.

Visual Literacy in Application

In the beginning of this chapter, we've shown was of "reading" an image, and thus we think of skills at visual interpretation as being related to visual literacy. Interpretations begin to form immediately when you see an image, and they develop over time as you notice more things in the image, learn more about the contexts that surround it, and connect it to existing opinions and ideas you have about what it depicts. But this process can be limited to a single image, or constrained by your own lack of knowledge about its subject(s). But honing your visual literacy, your skill and facility with "reading" these images deeply relies on additional elements. For one thing, you learn to recognize similarities repeated across multiple images; for example, Images 1.1 and 1.2 both have people looking at the camera. Your experience with other people tells you that the experience of seeing their faces is different from if you don't, and the practice of taking a photo differs between those two cases. The boys in Image 1.1 seem to have been photographed slightly more abruptly than the girls in Image 1.2 posed against a wall; how does a "candid" portrait differ from a staged one? The photos are both desaturated of color; what do they have in common with other photos you've seen of their color scheme and quality?

Also, visual literacy requires at first that you are thinking actively about these concepts. Over time, it becomes second nature to see an image and begin analyzing its features almost as fast as you gain your impressions of them. But at first, you must be self-conscious of these analyses, asking yourself how you "know" what you think you do about why and how an image has been produced in its particular way. This level of consideration is important to elevate our usual level of thinking about images, which we want to encourage because in the contemporary world, the visual bombardment is almost constant. Perhaps the most important part of visual literacy is being able to separate all the elements of a multimodal sign, and analyze each element in terms of their cultural meanings, before reassembling them to have a better idea of how the entire sign works. Those signs surround us, creating a lot of chaos to sort through, but ultimately leading to rich communicative environments.

Although we've done a fair bit of digging into our two key terms, please don't mistake what you are reading here for just an exercise in pure theory. It is grounded in theoretical principles, but the applications of learning more about visual literacy are many—in some cases obvious, in others, less so. Think of it this way: whenever you encounter a specific practice of looking, either in an academic or professional setting, you are required to have visual literacy for the field in question. This in turn makes you a stronger interpreter of what you see. Often, people simply memorize the information they're required to know without thinking about the underlying logic, by force of habit. How often do you stop and consider, why is it you look at things the way you do? But this kind of self-reflection enables academics and professionals in a wide range of disciplines to cross the gap from ordinary practitioners to people who can create compelling or persuasive visual content, or even shape the pursuit of knowledge in their fields of study.

Take art history, for example. A student *could*, through extensive practice, just memorize all the names, dates, and features of works of art they're interested in, passing their exams by rote and providing knowledgeable, but uninspired, essays on the topic. Or, by considering the visual context that surrounded each work of art as it was created, learning to regard those pieces as they would have been or could have been by their original audience, and recognizing how that regard changes over time, the student can unlock a much richer level of understanding. If you think of visuality as a kind of language with a literacy of its own, then a painting or sculpture that completely confounds its audience's visual expectation is as innovative as a work of experimental poetry that turns grammar on its head. Learning to interpret visual language helps the student of art history deduce much more thoroughly what an artist might have intended with their work. Our goal here is to equip you to do just that: a way to learn new ways of seeing, and a way to rethink the ones you already possess.

And this is just one example. Artists themselves benefit from being aware of how others will look at their work, as do filmmakers and graphic designers. We don't want to restrict our analysis to discrete objects, either: good architects and urban planners recognize how the meanings of *spaces* are perceived by people who occupy the buildings or neighborhoods they design. A journalist's research benefits by figuring out how their interview subjects see whatever it is they're talking about, as does the research of anthropologists and communication scholars. The entire world of marketing relies heavily on assumptions and findings about how consumers read advertisements. Video game developers need to put themselves in the gamer's place when laying out maps, and web designers must consider how different technological constraints will affect a customer's interaction with a website. Most people would probably agree that you can get a deeper understanding of others by walking a mile in their shoes; we encourage you to look for a while through their eyes. The possibilities are endless.

Ironically, visuality as a central issue in these disciplines is often overlooked, and people assume a naturalness to the interpretation of visual data when it is actually a well-developed and particular cultural practice. Just as with language, we are socialized into visual semiosis as young children so thoroughly that we hardly even realize it. When did you first realize that you should read text in a certain direction, or that certain colors were associated with certain genders, or that a dissolve effect in a film can signify the passage of time? None of these, nor the other thousands of elements we regularly read in the world around us, are the way they are out of necessity. (Yet they're not *entirely* random, either; you'd be hard-pressed to find a visual language that hasn't been built on top of another one.) By stepping back and not taking your own practices for granted, you will gain perspective into how they work. Then, you can apply that knowledge to become the best film critic (or whatever else) that you can.

We've prepared this handy table to show you a few examples of the myriad ways in which learning more about visuality can give you a deeper literacy in a few different disciplines:

Obviously, this is just the tip of the iceberg; anyone involved in one of these areas of study, or almost any other, could find a number of additional ways to apply the lessons of visual literacy

Area of Study	Relevant Concepts	Examples of Relevant Questions
Anthropology	semiotics of race; how we see and interpret the "other"	*How/Why have illustrations of non-"Western" peoples changed over time?*
Art, Art History	ideology; encoding/decoding; history of ways of seeing as ways of making new meaning	*What is the significance of using the color blue in paintings? How has that changed throughout history?*
Communication	visual and nonverbal communication	*Do visual impressions of others affect how one speaks to them?*
Education	learning styles; pedagogical methods	*What is the best way to use pictures to teach young children math?*
Game Design	user interface design; creating computer game maps	*When does an interface provide too much or too little information for players to navigate the game?*
Graphic Arts and Design	multimodality and persuasion; logos and branding	*When and how do dynamic infographics have more impact on an audience than simple graphs?*
Media Studies	visuality in the social imagination; critical literacy	*How do images of femininity and masculinity in popular media affect political campaigns?*

IMAGE 1.4 Visuality in many disciplines

to their work. With this introductory matter that you've read so far, what benefits can you think of for yourself? We find that questions like the examples in the right column are helpful when focusing ideas for research and other pursuits. Hopefully now you might ask, why did we choose to present this information in table form? How are the ideas organized within it, and why? Everything around you, including the content of this text, is fair game for digging into the visual logic, as well as the intentions of the creator(s) and your own preconceptions as a viewer.

Overall, the intention of this chapter is to demonstrate to you that seeing is a much more complicated process than most people give it credit for. Our goal is to train you to see more deeply, to be critical of the different ways of seeing people have (including your own), and to be able to apply your knowledge about what makes up the processes of visuality. Remember that there is always more *stuff* to dig into, and no one text could hope to cover the nearly infinite ways of seeing that are out there. As a result, we encourage you to do further outside reading when you can, especially if you have questions specific to your own field of experience—but we hope this text will do for an introduction, at least.

Exercises

1. Find six to ten images of cats, including photos, drawings, paintings, cartoons, etc. Try to put them in order of the most iconic (most closely resembles a real cat) to the least iconic (most abstract and least closely resembling a real cat). If in doubt, check out the assortment in Image 2.5 in the next chapter. Now ask yourself, what about the least iconic cat images still capture the idea or meaning of "cat"? How does your own experience with cats affect your answer to the last question?

2. Watch a short news video online. Which modes are carrying the greatest informational load—in other words, is the video, the audio, or the print on the screen the most important part that's informing you about the topic or event? Why do you think that mode was most important? What would the broadcast be like if the *least* important mode had the greatest informational load? What would the broadcast be like if one or more of the modes was missing?

3. Search the internet for an image of a city street scene from another country, where you've never been and where you wouldn't be able to speak the language. Locate all the physical signage you can; what can you understand? Note the use of color and symbolism. How many of the signs do you think are similar to ones you would encounter in your own part of the world? Try to find more information about the differences between the two.

For Further Exploration

Arcadia Publishing's *Images of America* series.

• Features over 5000 short, inexpensive photo books that tell local histories of regions and towns, as well as some photo books about specific industries, sport, and ethnic groups. Note the implications of their image-heavy book design, especially the covers.

Chandler, Daniel. (2007). *Semiotics: The Basics.* (Second edition). London: Routledge.

• Everything you always wanted to know about semiotics but were afraid to ask. Be sure to also do an internet search for Chandler's other offerings.

Freedman, Russell. (1994). *Kids at Work: Lewis Hine and the Crusade against Child Labor.* Boston, MA: Houghton Mifflin Harcourt.

• Collect the work of Lewis Hine, who documented child labor exploitation in his ultimately successful endeavor to change federal laws and workplace practices.

2
COGNITION AND VISION

Introduction

Part of what makes visuality and its implications unique is, of course, their foundation in the human system of vision. Even for scholars of the humanities and social sciences, it is helpful to learn the basics of biology, chemistry, physics, or whatever other natural science is relevant to your object of interest. In our case, a rudimentary understanding of how the eye works, and how the information it takes in is processed by the brain, is useful knowledge. When we talk about why a particular object in the world holds meaning for those who view it, or why certain colors, shapes, and spatial arrangements seem to catch our attention, this gets us part of the way there.

Primates and Vision

Certain primates such as monkeys, apes and humans have a special visual adaptation called the *fovea centralis*, which is a densely concentrated area of cone-shaped light receptors on the retina at the back of the eye (take a look at Image 2.1). Primate foveae (excluding those of most prosimians) are very well-developed, and primates see color and contrast in a different and often more refined way than other mammals. We are trichromatic animals, whose cones are adapted to see pigments along the light spectrum that include violet, green, and yellow-green, which are respectively short, medium, and longer medium wavelengths. This adaptation is probably directly related to our success at foraging for orange and yellow fruits against green foliage backgrounds.

In conjunction with other parts and functions of the eye, the specialization of the fovea also allows primates to do things

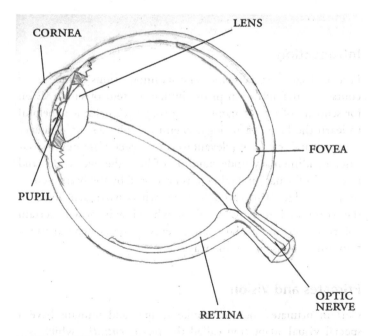

IMAGE 2.1 Diagram of eye

like move safely when tossing their hands and feet from tree to tree. For humans, the fovea helps us to evaluate very sharply the detailed and complicated visual information while climbing trees, hunting and gathering, driving cars, playing sports and games, watching movies, conducting lab experiments, and drawing and reading. Such sharp central vision is undoubtedly part of why we gravitate toward the development of visual cultures, where making finely tuned visual distinctions become part of how we process information. Much of this visual processing is automatic—that is, we do it without conscious effort, but it is important to remember that automaticity can be learned as well as be inborn.

Another adaptation, *stereoscopic vision*, allows us to collect incredibly sophisticated information about the dimensions of the world around us. By having our eyes relatively wide apart but on the same plane in the skull, when we look forward, we automatically compare what the right and left eye sees. That comparison of viewing angles, along with our skills at depth perception from the *gestalt* tendencies discussed below, allows us to judge distance with very high accuracy. Note that humans who lose sight in one eye can still imagine three-dimensional sight, but their acuity in estimating three-dimensional space tends to diminish.

DOGS, HUMANS, AND THE LEFT BIAS GAZE FOR FACES

Scientists have been exploring what it means that humans and primates in general tend to have a "left face bias" when it comes to gazing upon each other's faces, always casting our eyes to the left as when we newly see someone's face. It is almost certain because negative emotions tend to show most clearly upon the right side of faces (i.e., on our left when the person is facing us), when people are feeling angry, anxious, sad, or volatile. It stands to reason that primates would've had an adaptive advantage if they could extremely quickly assess if an oncoming conspecific (meaning a member of their own species) were about to attack them, and thus, we as primates probably evolved this ability in the deep past. It's also been established that the contemporary primates like rhesus monkeys also have left gaze bias for both monkey faces and human faces. Indeed, the genetically endowed tendency for left gaze bias can easily be demonstrated in very young human babies, who automatically direct their gaze toward the right sides of faces of the people they encounter.

What about when the subjects aren't conspecific, and aren't humans or monkeys? Experiments have been conducted with domesticated dogs, where they are presented with novel and familiar faces and their eyes tracked while they gather visual information on the humans before them. They also have a left face bias when looking at humans, but when they look at conspecifics, or other dogs, they do not have this bias. Dogs were domesticated perhaps 20–30 thousand years ago, so their sensitivity to our expressions is not too much of a surprise. It's much more than likely that those dogs who succeeded most as companions to humans were those who had developed the same ability to gauge our moods quickly.

However, as babies, all the visual information humans receive is initially unrecognizable "visual noise"; both rod and cone (respectively, light and color) receptors are not fully developed while the size and shape of babies' retinas change as the skull develops after birth. By 8 weeks, eyes start to focus and at 3 months, babies begin to track various stimuli with their eyes. By the 5th month, depth perception starts to be detectable in infants and soon after, hand-eye coordination starts to develop. All through this developmental sequence, babies are learning to interpret color and light contrasts to grasp what is foreground and background, and to make sense of which objects in front of them deserve primary focus, both visually and intellectually.

Visual Development and Human Cognition

Vision and perception—by which we mean the brain's ability to organize data about our surroundings, recognizing, and categorizing them—are interrelated cognitive skills. As babies develop the ability to discern movement, color, distance, and so forth, they simultaneously begin to perceive objects *as objects*, as well as the relationships among them. One way we know this is because blind infants take quite a bit longer than sighted children to develop perceptual skills, and as they do (through auditory stimuli), the perceptual skills of blind children develop within the brain's perceptual visual centers. In other words, perception has a strong link to visuality, although other senses can take over and use the visual processing mechanism to develop perceptual abilities. Further proof of the direct link between visuality and perceptual development is that deaf children who learn signing will develop perceptual skills to identify and process information at the same rate as hearing children. That is, spoken language and its cognitive centers in the brain *initially* have less to do with perception than vision and the visual centers for processing information in the brain.

HOW DOES HUMAN EYE MOVEMENT "WORK"?

On average, a person will shift their gaze about 3 times per second, coordinating head, eye, and body movements to bring visual information to that crucial area of the fovea where we can see with clarity and sharpness. These jumps of the eyes that focus our attention on stimuli, called saccades, tell us a bit about how the brain functions.

There are two related processes in how eye movement is understood. First is the process of collecting indirect or "bottom up" input, in which the eye seeks out a stimulus with intense speed, and in an automatic sort of way. We literally take in and process visual information without even trying. For example, we are hard-wired to ignore blanks space or spaces without stimuli. The second process in how human eye gaze gathers information is about direct or "top down" information intake. Even in eye movements as fast as 3 times per second, we are somewhat consciously directing our gaze, evaluating information, and integrating that information with what we know previously. This sort of top down gaze direction is one that is oriented toward salience: what in the visual field can tell you something you want or need to know? The intentionality of this second process allows us to gather visual information coherently and usefully.

Really, both stimuli and salience can be operative at the same time. Psychologists of reading use eye-tracker machines to figure out how children get information from text as they learn to read, paying attention to both the "bottom up," automatic jumps of the eye as children learn to take in stimuli from print, and the uptake from more deliberate jumps back and forth, as readers align previously read information with new information. Thus, eye tracking is one of the central ways that cognitive scientists can determine, rather literally, how humans think and learn, integrating information by using incredibly fast, precise, and complicated visual interactions with our environment.

Gestalt and Vision

Gestalt theory is a systematic approach to human perception, based largely on psychological experiments around how people fill in missing bits and pieces in a visual field; the basic idea is that the whole is greater than the sum of its parts. As mentioned above, human development for sighted individuals involves developing a way to interpret visual information within perceptual systems, so that we can construct useful mental maps of what is around us. When some of that information is obscured, we rely on logic, previous experience, or just assumption to overcome that gap, which is called *amodal perception*. For example, if you see a partial glimpse of something or encounter a partly obscured object you will perceive of it as a whole (or *plenum*, to use the technical term) object even though you cannot see all of it. This kind of "depth ordering" is part of what makes us susceptible to optical illusions such as a Kanizsa triangle, where we imagine a white triangle among three partially eaten pies (see Image 2.2). Our tendency to

IMAGE 2.2 Kanisza triangle

fill in the missing lines shows a cognitive bias toward recognizing completed or whole figures—in this case, a triangle.

Figure and *ground* are also important concepts for grasping how people order visual information. We have a strong tendency to order the visual world around us by orienting items with respect to a *ground*, meaning the item furthest away, usually placing or perceiving the ground toward the bottom or the background of the image. The *figure*, on the other hand, is perceived as being in the front, the object of movement, or otherwise foregrounded. The poster from Amnesty International (see Image 2.3) illustrates this by forcing us to alternate what the figure and ground are, in order to perceive two kinds of hands. Further complicating our sense of depth, we also use

IMAGE 2.3 Amnesty International, 1985 campaign logo

color to perceive foreground (darker), middle ground (lighter), and background (lightest), as is widely taught in landscape drawing classes. Notice how the outstretched hand figures in the image play with our sense of foreground and background, light and dark, to make a compelling symbol for the work that Amnesty International does rescuing and advocating for refugees in crisis.

Because we so readily fill in the gaps in our perception with assumed details, and look for orderings of objects, it can be difficult to realize how often we do it. Gestalt theorists often talk in terms of "laws" that describe these tendencies. An important idea for grasping the interplay of cognition and visuality is the rush for *closure*—that is, our belief that we have gathered all the necessary information about something in our visual field—that we all experience. Closure leads us to automatically fill in the gaps, both in vision and in cognition. When confronted with a picture of half a dog adjacent to a table, we get visual closure by imagining a whole dog behind the table. (The idea of closure is extremely important for understanding visual narrative, and comics, which we will discuss in Chapter 4 in some detail.)

Other gestalt principles worth knowing about are ideas such as *proximity* (when we perceive similar objects near each other, we perceive them as a group) and *symmetry* (the tendency toward perceiving objects as being symmetrical, or symmetrically arranged). Sometimes we are *too* good at finding shapes to group together; the phenomenon of *pareidolia* refers to when we see forms like faces in a car's grill or objects in the shapes of a cloud. Humans and primates seem to be particularly attuned to faces, perhaps for evolutionary reasons, but also as a trait that defines individuals in a social species. However strongly these processes affect us, they have implications for everything from child psychology to public safety, from brand logos to accessible text and web design. But more broadly, they remind us that the world around us is cluttered with objects, and part of the realm of vision and visuality is how we order that chaos.

Optics and Human Perception of Moving Pictures

Unsurprisingly, our technologies of vision are adapted to our own eyesight. For example, since humans will process 24 frames per second visually as a continuous moving image, that is more or less the standard minimum for motion pictures (although there are differences between how celluloid film and digital formats handle this; see also Chapter 4). This ability to perceive sequential images as continuous movement is called *persistence of vision*. Early motion pictures didn't always get the optimal frames per second ratio correct, and images from early movies can seem herky-jerky as a result. Nevertheless, because of persistence of vision, we are able to "see" the continuous movement in them. Likewise, if you spin a zoetrope too quickly, the images will solidify and or/ disappear, but again, through our natural persistence, they will be perceived as a persistent visual object, or a distinct blur. Indeed, Italian physicist Vasco Ronchi points out that an image can be defined as merely a recognizable aberration or nonuniformity in the light patterns on a surface; when recognition ends, the image ends for us humans, even if it's still there and detectable through something other than the human eye. For dogs and cats, however, the "flicker rate" at which light can be determined and processed through the eye is greater than humans; this means that a TV screen updating pixelated lines at the rate of 60 times per second are perceived as normal moving images to humans, but to dogs and cats, the screen would appear to flicker.

Modern theories of optics starting in the 17th century with Rene Descartes, which have to do with lenses, light, and projection, were part of a new science of understanding how we see phenomena in space and time. They led directly to the development of greater telescopes, eyeglasses and contacts, photography, motion pictures, microscopy, and so on. In a sense, both the projection of images and the use of optics to see what we cannot in our natural state, are extensions of human cognition. The interplay between our visual and cognitive limitations, and how we get around them, directly influenced the philosophy and the machines we use to expand upon or to even break those limits.

Differences of Vision and Visuality

The visual system we have described is, of course, an idealized one. Most people don't have perfect vision, and even fewer maintain it throughout their lives. While we are primarily concerned in this book with social and cultural issues that shape perception, we would be remiss not to mention the physiological as well. Several disorders of the eye are so common as to be part of normal human variation: nearsightedness and farsightedness can appear in childhood, and are generally treated with glasses or contact lenses. As the eye grows older, it weakens and can degenerate or develop cataracts, sometimes necessitating surgery—and of course, diseases are possible at any age (see box Responding to Cataracts). All of these ailments, and often their treatments, can fundamentally change the way that the ocular portion of the vision system works, and how the data a person receives through the eye is interpreted.

RESPONDING TO CATARACTS

Cataracts are one of the most common vision problems for the elderly, affecting nearly everyone over the age of 65, although the rate is a bit variable across countries and genetic groups. Vision becomes blurry or filmy, and "halos" might appear around light, especially at night. Cataracts can also affect color recognition, a consideration for art historians considering the changes to a painter's work over time (see Chapter 3). All of this is due to proteins in the lens of the eye changing and clouding over. Sometimes children

---

are born with cataracts, or people develop them as part of a congenital disease, but the leading causes are aging, diabetes, and certain types of sun exposure. Cataracts are treatable, but without medical intervention, they lead to ever-worsening visual impairment, and are the number one cause of blindness in the world.

Procedures for fixing cataracts go back to the ancient Greeks, who would whack the lens of the eye to break up the hardest of protein deposits and restore at least some light vision to the patient. In the 1750s in France, surgeon Jacques Daviel experimented with some success at removing and replacing bad lenses surgically. But in the last 20 years, laser surgery and tiny foldable prosthetic lenses became key to the now widespread, delicate (but relatively simple) procedure to "cure" cataracts. It involves making a small incision, and removing the old lens, as well as any protein deposits left behind, while then inserting a new synthetic lens. Since the surgery is performed on an outpatient basis, healing is relatively quick—usually 1 or 2 weeks, and the procedure is a success about 95% of the time. So why the high rate of blindness?

Nations and regions with older overall populations have higher demand for cataract surgeries, and of course, the clinics, equipment, and ophthalmological surgeons required to do them. Probably more than 20 million people worldwide have cataract related blindness and numbers grow slightly higher each year as the average age of the population in many countries rises. The growth rate won't be reduced until the demand is lessened. Sadly, capacity doesn't always meet demand. Even in the United States, a complicated dance of billing, insurance, and the relative availability of surgical facilities and surgeons leads to some people, even in the middle class, not always getting the cataract treatments they need. Interestingly, however, the presence of just a few physicians, nurses, and some international training assistance can lead to the development of clinics like the Eye Foundation Hospital Group in Lagos, Nigeria. This medical group was established as a non-profit arm of a for-profit clinic in the early 2000s and continues to build capacity in Nigeria for training physicians and nurses in vision treatment and medical technology (Bogunjoko et al., 2018).

Such efforts don't completely solve the problem; Nigeria lacks enough trained ophthalmologists, and those available generally live in the large cities. (This urban concentration of doctors is a common problem in many nations.) City clinics can't serve the entire local population, affordability remains a problem, and residents in remote areas without the means to travel or pay probably spend their later years with impaired vision, or even blind. These challenges remind us that no matter how much new technology we develop around vision and visuality, the broader social issues of access to healthcare are paramount in making technology serve the people.

More subtle are conditions like color-blindness, which has a variety of types and causes. We often take our color vision for granted. How do you imagine your experience of the world (and in keeping with our theme, your experience of complex signs that involve color like stop lights or color-coded maps) might be different if you couldn't see certain colors? Another meaningful condition is *synesthesia*, wherein one kind of sensory input triggers another. One of the most common forms is *grapheme-color synesthesia*, where a text's individual letters and numbers are perceived to have colors associated with them, regardless of the color of the ink on the page or pixels on the screen. On the one hand, the riot of colors that might appear when a synesthete attempts to read can be highly distracting; on the other hand, the association can be an aid to remembering words and names. Neither of these conditions is especially rare, and perhaps you, the reader, even have some degree of one of them.

Then there are disorders of visuality itself, by which we mean those that have less to do with how information is taken in than how it is processed in the mind. A good example is the condition *prosopagnosia*, or "face blindness," where an individual has trouble recognizing faces. Those who suffer from it often rely on memorized cues—this person wears glasses and has a mole on her chin, that person has a beard and a scar on his forehead—to get by, and many people with the condition report having to learn to cope with the anxiety or even fear that strikes them when they cannot recognize people whom they should. It has been suggested that this condition stems from an inability to create a gestalt perception of all the elements of a face, something that most people are able to construct without thinking. Or, we might consider *aphantasia*, a term coined fairly recently to describe an inability to visualize the imaginary—blindness of the mind's eye. Those with the condition cannot conjure up many memories, dreams, or hypothetical situations in terms of images; they cannot "picture" things the way most of us do easily. And the constellation of causes and types of full visual hallucinations are practically limitless; unlike physical deformities of the eye or injuries to the brain, they can be much harder to pinpoint.

It should be mentioned that for many conditions like this, those who have them don't necessarily recognize anything "abnormal" about their visuality, and many get by just fine. The word "disorder" implies that there is a right way and a wrong way to see; we would argue that as much as the meanings of symbols and signs are culturally constructed, so too are the "default" ways of seeing. Obviously, if an individual's way differs to the point that it disrupts their interactions with others and ability to function in society, that can be a problem, but often more of a social one than a medical one. Sometimes a person with one of these conditions doesn't even recognize that they have an issue until much later in life, when they realize that the visuality of others works differently. This raises the question: what is the connection between the stimulus and response of the eye—light hitting cells, electricity firing along the optic nerve—and the *experience* of seeing? What happens when a color-blind person or synesthetic person discovers that what they believe to be a normal, everyday experience differs from that of everyone around them? (This is not exactly a hypothetical question, as many people have written detailed accounts about those moments.)

Philosophers of perception have long debated the nature of subjective experiences like these, called **qualia**, and how truly universal or individual they are. For our purposes here, it will be enough to say that almost nobody has a "perfect" visual system that endures throughout their lifespan. Even if we allow that some group of people are close enough that we can say they represent the baseline of what we mean when we talk about human vision, there is enough difference between them in terms of culture, history, and personality to ensure that everyone's interpretations of visual data will be unique.

Artists Seeing Differently

What is the impact of atypical, or altered, vision and visuality for an artist? On the one hand, painters and illustrators depend on their ability to translate their way of seeing into an artifact that others can appreciate. On the other hand, we often expect them to have an unexpected point of view, and the works of artists with conditions like those described here can be a valuable reference for understanding those perceptions.

The work of Monet is often used as a "before and after" example. He developed cataracts in his 70s, had them removed

IMAGE 2.4 Claude Monet, Japanese Bridge paintings; top from 1899; bottom from 1918 to 1924

several years later, and painted for a few more years before his death at age 86. While the majority of his later work is known for its diffuse quality, he progressed from "natural" colors and shapes to much more abstract pieces tinted red (since cataracts tint the vision red—see Image 2.4—and eventually blue). Biographers have speculated that after his operation, he was able to perceive ultraviolet light, and attempted to depict that in his paintings.

Another commonly cited case is that of Louis Wain, whose pictures of anthropomorphic cats are used to demonstrate the effect of shifts in mental health (in Wain's case, most likely from schizophrenia). Wain's earlier work is more naturalistic, while

IMAGE 2.5 Cats, by Louis Wain

his later drawings transform into abstract, colorful patterns that are vaguely catlike. It remains unclear whether there was a definite progression from conventional to psychedelic modes of seeing after he was committed; the pictures were undated, and there is evidence that Wain was painting in both styles until late in his life. Still, it is plausible to say that he indeed had an alternative way of seeing that manifests in his art (Image 2.5).

The medical histories of other historical figures remain obscure. In her volume *Scivias*, the 12th-century abbess Hildegard von Bingen documents a series of her religious visions. Various scholars (notably neurologist Oliver Sacks) point out that both the descriptions and the accompanying illustrations show characteristics of the symptoms of persistent migraine, such as "scintillating" shapes and colors. Similarly, it has often been claimed that Vincent Van Gogh, who suffered from ill health all his life, had one or more conditions that led to his penchant for painting "haloes" and yellow tints. Yet there is no clear evidence for this, and there may be no correlation between his health and his art.

In many cases, it is hard to know for sure which of these features directly represent a medical condition, and how much is simply artistic license. As the definition of "art" itself (not to mention the definition of "illness") shifts through time and place, it becomes even more difficult to say for certain. Nevertheless, artists are uniquely equipped to demonstrate how personal vision and visuality can be—yet another valuable quality they and their work possess.

Color and Culture

As we've already suggested, the meanings we associate with colors are more culturally constructed than anything else. True, there is some biological basis: the cone cells of the eye are most sensitive to certain colors and wavelengths, and some colors tend to stand out more than others in different conditions. But if you are asked to describe what the color red *means* to you, it is unlikely that you will describe it in scientific terms, something like: "the property of objects that reflect the longest wavelengths of visible light."

There is an ongoing, cross-disciplinary debate about the relationship between colors and how they are named in different languages, most famously researched in the 1960s by Brent Berlin and Paul Kay. In their initial study, the two researchers noted that when it comes to "basic" color terms in the languages they studied, there tends to be a certain progression in which color terms come into being and are used as languages develop over time. So, for example, a young or newly forming language will develop terms for "dark/cool" and "light/warm" colors before they develop a word for "red." They must have words for "green" and "yellow" before there can be a word for "blue," etc. Over the last several decades, Berlin and Kay themselves have continually revised their hypotheses to account for languages that don't exactly fit this pattern, while numerous linguists, anthropologists, and cognitive scientists have set out to test them. These experiments are often put in the context of the **linguistic relativity** (sometimes called the *Sapir-Whorf hypothesis*, after two linguists who developed the idea), which means that the language a person speaks shapes the way they think—and therefore, how they see.

There are few concepts that have so polarized scholars across the humanities, social sciences, and natural sciences. For those on the "strong relativity" end of the spectrum, they believe language tends to shape thought more often than not; for those on the "weak relativity" end, they acknowledge that there is a relationship, but not one that determines how we think. Color provides a touchstone case: do we all see the same colors in the same way, if our languages have different ways of handling the spectrum? There are extreme versions of this argument, such as the contention that Ancient Greeks had not yet evolved the vision apparatus to see color, based on descriptions like the "wine-dark sea" and "bronze sky" in Homer's *Odyssey*. Of course, an alternative is simply that these color words were not based on hue, like ours, but on other characteristics like brightness or saturation of color, or simply established metaphors different from those in our language. (English often uses "green" to describe someone who looks ill, but it would be an extraordinary illness that caused someone to actually, fully turn green). A more recent example comes from the Himba people of Namibia, who have the color words *buru* (including some greens and blue) and *dambu* (including other greens, red, and brown). It has been suggested that as a result, their eyes and brains are able to quickly distinguish among shades of green, but have a lot of trouble distinguishing green from blue.

The reason we use the word "suggested" in the Himba example is that at least one of the experiments popularly said to demonstrate this cultural color-blindness has since been shown to be poorly designed, and inconclusive. Yet stories like this crop up regularly in the media, and the internet goes wild—why? It may, unfortunately, reflect a subtle tendency that all kinds of relativity study bring out: cultural chauvinism, or even racism. Note that in the Berlin-Kay progression above, English and most European languages, of course, have all the basic color terms listed. It would be easy for an untrained person to read this and assume this means that English speakers are among the most "evolved," at least when it comes to color vision (notwithstanding the fact that some languages, like Russian, seem to have even more basic terms). The history of science, and Western anthropology more than most others, has some pretty grim chapters that modern scholars are still trying to overcome. We urge you to avoid a trap that catches many people who don't have the opportunity to study these issues more deeply: do not confuse *difference* with *evaluation*. To put it more simply, just because languages, cultures, and the people who embody have different ways of seeing and describing the world, that doesn't mean that one is inherently "better" than another.

Perhaps this can be seen more clearly if we return to our opening question in this section: what does the color red *mean*? Well, depending on where you're from in the world, it could mean *emergency*, or *good fortune*, or *love* and *passion*. Localizing a color in certain broad contexts such as religion (*cardinals' robes* in Roman Catholicism vs. *monks' robes* in some sects of Buddhism) or neighborhoods (*red-light districts*) can make a difference. Objects can similarly add information: if you're looking at a carpet outside a theatre, red might mean *VIP*, but if you're looking at a traffic light, it probably means *stop*. To a color-blind person, red might not have much meaning at all, while a synesthete, or a student of American literature, might connect it to *the letter A*. You also might have a personal association with it that nobody else has.

This is all to demonstrate that beyond having different ways of describing color, people also have different ways of *interpreting* color. The two processes are not the same, yet they both matter to visuality, from the individual all the way up to the communal. And even though we tend to think of our associations as a given, even within a culture, they can change over time. Consider the color red in politics: the American student might be surprised to learn that the concept of the Republican "Red State" was not solidified until as recently as the 2000 presidential election (based on how vote tallies were represented in televised news graphics). Or the clothing of infants: up until the mid-20th century, pink was the boys' color, since it was a shade of red, the most "energetic" color. We mean to destabilize these color schemes not to confuse you, but to help you question your own visuality, and the concept of visuality as a fixed value. The reasons you see things the way you do may not be the reasons you think.

Maps and Cognition of Space

Maps arguably affect cognition, too: when we integrate knowledge from maps into our understanding of the spaces of the world, we are joining that information to our personal, direct experiences of navigating the world. Learning about the symbology of maps, as well as the systems that maps portray (longitude and latitude, standardized measurements of distance, etc.) also changes how we experience space; have you ever looked at a map and said about a place, "I didn't realize it was that close"? Without having integrated the visual language of maps into the way we think, that sentence would be absurd!

The historical ideology of maps—for instance, navigational maps distorting relative placement and proportions of landmasses, subtly reinforcing the idea of European dominance—is outside the direct scope of this chapter. But the question of how symbols in maps represent reality is crucial to understanding how maps create shared perceptual understandings of the world. It seems an odd way to think about it, but maps are a technology that has been developed from generations of visual, geometrical, and navigational knowledge. By both creating and recording systems of navigation like latitude and longitude, maps enabled explorers to travel vast distances through unknown spaces across a *round* Earth.

Maps serve all sorts of different functions, but one of them has always been as a navigational tool. Briefly, prior to the idea of latitude and longitude, maps were involved with trying to record "the shortest distance between two points" (*distance*) situated against the cardinal directions North/South/East/West (*bearing*), in order to figure out where places and travelers were (hoping perhaps to be able to stop in time before falling off the edge). The problem was that long distance lines of travel that held north to a steady position, without appreciation of the curvature of the planet, would ultimately send sailors and land explorers in uncharted areas off course. To fix this, the Flemish cartographer Mercator laid out his map of the world with a series of vertical (longitude lines) and horizontal (latitude lines) stripes with related axes across an imagined sphere (rather than a grid). These two lines could be used in tandem to circumnavigate a world along routes that had not previously been taken. Thus, a specific kind of knowledge born of a visualization technology came to characterize the West's entire visual, spatial, and perceptual understanding of the shapes and spaces of the globe.

Likewise, in a much more mundane but still very important example of how people share mental ideas of visual space, consider how we describe space when we give directions to someone. Without even knowing it, we tend to organize space in our minds in a visual and linguistic manner that is both efficient and easy to share. For example, when describing a house layout, we will almost always start at the entrance, imagining a "tour" and telling our audience about main rooms first, and satellite rooms (closets, pantries, nooks) in relationship to the main room they connect to. We will also mention what is on the "left" or the "right" or at the "back" while replicating our sense of a tour, and somehow, or hearers can visualize pretty well what we are saying. This kind of visual and perceptual storage in memory is so strong that many people can describe map-like layouts of places they have only been once or twice, and many years previous. For a species without instinctual abilities to orient direction of travel, this kind of complex visual cognition is one of the keys to our long-term development, individually and communally.

Exercises

1. Celebrated British painter Sargy Mann stated: "It seems that blindness has given me the freedom to use color in ways that I would not have dared to when I could see." There are several short documentaries and trailers on the web about artists who are visually impaired, as well as artists who make art for the visually impaired. Some suggestions besides Sargy Mann include: Keith Salmon, John Bramblett, Rachel Gadsden or search for others. Find a video featuring a visual artist with visual impairment: Why do you think these artists talk about increasing freedom to use color in new and creative ways? Why do you think blind and seeing people wish to communicate through art to each other and across their differences?

2. Go to testmybrain.org or other similar site that offers a face memory test and try it individually or as a group. Answer the following: during the face memory test, how were you trying to "learn" the faces that you saw, and what does that tell you about how humans recognize faces? What makes identification easier or more difficult? If you had (or really do have) prosopagnosia, how would you enjoy television and movies? How would you remember people in your mind's eye? (Note also that issues of race and face recognition are brought up in Chapter 9).

3. Try to explain to someone how to get to a novel location, taking notes on how spatial cognition is represented in language that is both visual (look for the statue of a big dragon the corner), fixed reference (keep downtown on your right; head west), and about time or space (walk straight for 15 minutes). What kinds of cognitive effort does this take and what makes navigation harder or easier—visual, spatial, or other ideas? What about following smartphone mapping functions?

For Further Exploration

Kay, Paul, et al. (2010). *The World Color Survey*. Stanford, CA: CSLI Publications.

* An update of the original color terms study by the authors and their colleagues, accounting for some new theories and data from the field.

Mann, Peter (Producer and Director). (2006). *Sargy Mann* (documentary film). Peter Mann Pictures, United Kingdom.

* Short documentary about British painter Sargy Mann who slowly lost his eyesight but continued to find new ways to produce visual art.

Livingstone, Margaret, & D. H. Hubel (2008). *Vision and art: the biology of seeing*. New York: Abrams. *ISBN 978081099554*.

* Prominent neurobiologist explains how we see classic works of art.

Sacks, Oliver. (2010). Face-Blind: Why are some of us terrible at recognizing faces? *New Yorker)*, August 23, pp. 36–43.

* An autobiographic journey with a face-blind neurologist.

3

VISUAL HISTORY, VISUAL CULTURE, IDEOLOGY

Introduction

We can only guess what first inspired early humans to depict the world around them as they were exercising new kinds of consciousness. While archaeology has attempted to interpret and contextualize the wealth of artifacts uncovered worldwide since its beginnings as a formal discipline in the 19th century, the reason for that initial leap from simply observing the world around us to creating artwork as a representational *way of seeing* remains unclear. Maybe it was the new kinds of social organization that arose from new roles within hunter gatherer groups. Perhaps they had a need for visual aids while storytelling; cave paintings tend to show people collectively engaged in a hunt. Certainly social and economic change is associated with the development of new forms and content in art since our beginnings. But how did the first artists make it clear to others that what they had created was meant to reflect something in the world?

Visual recording could simply be an ingrained part of how humans transmit their culture across generations, the first widespread instance of the cognitive shift we still see now when adults show children a picture and say, "This is a ..." However it happened—and it has happened again and again throughout human history—the fact remains that representation is a crucial part of human cultures, from sketching lines and figures in the sand to creating elaborate iconography on consumer products. The system and its elements change from group to group, but with perhaps a few exceptions, a heritage of visual meaning-making can be found everywhere.

Examining the history of art and representation is not without its pitfalls. Many early archaeologists often considered their findings in light of the common scientific ideas of the time that separated people into "primitive" and "civilized" categories: older was necessarily simpler, and Western was necessarily better. We still struggle against these kinds of beliefs, but with a bit of reflection and examination it becomes clear that even the simplest-seeming artwork can have the potential to be very sophisticated in terms of how it reflects human visuality. For example, the earliest cave paintings have perspective and the suggestion of motion just as a lot of art in contemporary times does. We also surmise that the portrayals of hunters and animals in caves would have served a very different social symbolic role than, for example, paintings in Egyptian tombs (see Image 3.1). However, even as we acknowledge and try to minimize our own cultural biases, we face another dilemma: how can we really know that a certain work means what we think it means, or more importantly, how do we know we are seeing it in the way its original creators saw it? Interpreting the products of artists long gone is especially challenging for prehistoric cultures of which we have no record other than a few scattered objects with ambiguous functions. But more recent images in the history of representation are also subject to this problem of discerning the maker's intent and the users' experiences of the artifact in their

IMAGE 3.1 Line drawing of a prehistoric cave painting, Valltorta-Gasulla, Spain (about 8–9,000 years ago); compare the presentation of bodies and movement in this painting to the ancient Egyptian image in 3.2

time and place. The way we look at things is as much a product of our local and personal circumstances as it is a product of the biological systems of visuality and cognition that we've already discussed.

This chapter provides a few historical examples of how people in earlier eras saw and understood visual signs, in the semiotic sense (see Chapter 1) in their own environments. We also explore a few religious, political, and economic influences on visual elements in human culture. These influences reflect and refract who people are within their time and place. We draw on at least a few distinctive visual cultures from art history, but our focus on Western visual forms is a reflection of our own backgrounds and ways of seeing. Still, as long as we acknowledge the bias inherent in our points of view and consider the relationship between what we cover here and the vast array of other works out there, these examples are useful for understanding contemporary visual media. We also want to remind you that while contemporary visual culture all over the world has at least some global connections to postindustrial European and American traditions, visual material from other cultures has in turn been incorporated or appropriated by the West for centuries.

All images must be situated in a particular time, place, and context. Our purpose here is to highlight some of the different representations in history that require different kinds of visuality. What does each piece tell you? Think about how your own experience shapes your interpretations of the work, and consider how the experiences of the creator(s) and their original audience might change the way they saw things? What was the kind of information they received and how does your idea of their idea affect your uptake of information?

Interpreting Ancient Art

Perhaps the best-known body of ancient art is that of Egypt in the Pharaonic period. Its conventions are so, well, *conventional* that they are instantly recognizable: the unique profile view of human figures, their scale based on relative importance, the use of symbolism, etc. Tomb walls in pyramids and in the graves of the Valley of the Kings are densely decorated with art that represents connections to the Egyptian divine, records the lifetime deeds of the deceased, and depicts scenes of the bountiful harvests and riches that are to be part of the afterlife. Egyptian statuary has figures with animal attributes or holding ritually significant objects that would have been instantly recognizable to an observer. What do these artworks communicate? To archaeologists, they may represent records of Egyptian society, beliefs, and history, but to the ancient Egyptians, they further reinforced what the viewers already knew and assumed about life in their world.

Consider also the image of Egyptian royal craftsmen in Image 3.2. Although we tend to think of Egyptian art as static profiles, a closer look shows us that often Egyptian painters rotated the plane of the body in the creation of their two-dimensional images in order to show us as much of the body as possible. We see both legs, torsos, and chests from the front (in some paintings you can also see all of the fingers and two toes). This convention in Egyptian art was established in the early dynasties and continued for over a thousand years, executed by anonymous painters whose work reflected religious functions. The body was a sacred object, and preserving as much of it as

IMAGE 3.2 Facsimile, Craftsmen, Tomb of Nebamun and Ipuky, 1390–1349 B.C. featuring "Twisted Perspective," or the composite view in Egyptian art

possible in both representation and physical form—on papyrus, on a wall, in a sculpture, and especially as a mummy—was a central task in the overlapping pursuits of religion and art in Egyptian life. The anonymity of Egyptian painters and carvers was also part of the visual culture, where obeying convention as closely as possible (rather than setting oneself apart) was the closest one could come to the divine. Nevertheless, we do know that scribes, who were also artists, had relatively high status in Egyptian society; their work was deemed important for the smooth functioning of everyday life, sanctified by religion. Hence, to read and understand Egyptian visual culture first requires at least a basic understanding of some elements of Egyptian religious semiotics (i.e., how signs and the conventions for combining them create sacred meaning) and its producers.

But just as ethnic groups have different languages that set them apart from their neighbors, so too do they have different (even if only slightly) visual languages that require the same patience to fully learn. Think of it this way: when you look across visual cultures, you see with an "accent." Unless you are an ancient Egyptian (an unlikely proposition), it is not possible for you to look at those wall paintings or sculptures in the exact same way that they did, no matter how much training you might have. These images will create a different set of impressions and aspects of the world for you than they did for their original audience, although sometimes the similarities between what audiences perceive can be striking. Note that the conventions of Egyptian art changed very little throughout most of its history; perhaps its *timelessness* is a quality that both the original and modern viewer could agree on. In any case, it's always tempting to interpret the visual through your own experience first, and certainly it's easier than doing background research on whatever image you're encountering. Moreover, those personal and highly subjective impressions arise almost instantly, and are nearly impossible to suppress.

Rather than allowing these impressions to overtake any other contextual clues, we urge you to use what anthropologists call *reflexivity*: a self-awareness of your own position in your social and cultural world. If an Egyptian sculpture strikes you as "conservative," or "odd," or "primitive," ask yourself *why*. When you react strongly to any image, ask who it was made for, and where you are placed relative to that person, in terms of status. And most of all, look for the discrepancy—or perhaps the continuity—between your values and those of the time and place in which the work was created.

To give another example of contextualizing ancient art, when the Roman city of Pompeii (buried by volcanic ash in 79 A.D.) was unearthed in the 18th century, excavators were famously shocked at the number of small artifacts shaped like genitalia, as well as the frescoes with erotic themes they found, not to mention the frequent graffiti talking about certain citizens' sexual prowess. Romans had often been held up in history as paragons of civic duty and propriety, but as the frescoes of Pompeii were discovered by archaeologists in the Enlightenment era, the early Christian criticisms of the Empire as decadent and depraved began to seem more understandable. Yet Pompeii, its daily life, its people, and their morals had been gone for nearly 2000 years, and only had their surviving artwork, architecture. and remnants of their material culture to offer a counterpoint. Eventually it became clear that not *all* the citizens of the city were sex-crazed maniacs, but simply that Roman painters were much less inclined to see sex as a taboo subject. Moreover, the frescoes were so common because they brightened up otherwise drab, dark rooms in Roman houses. Genital-shaped objects illustrate their central role as talismans to a society that placed family and reproduction among the highest virtues. Reflexivity demands that we approach all these images on their own terms, and failing that, we at least recognize the limits of our own preconceptions.

Five Thousand Years of Text

Egyptian iconography paired images of humans, animals, and religious objects with parallel representations in the form of *hieroglyphs* (a Greek word meaning "sacred carvings"), which the Egyptians called *medunetjer* or "gods' words/divine writing." This was a pictographic form of writing used for moments that demanded honor for religion or the afterlife, and therefore were limited almost exclusively to royal and state monuments, or to religious settings. As with the conventions of figurative art, the stylized forms of religious writing were very long-lived, lasting from the 3rd millennium B.C. until around the 4th century A.D. with minimal changes.

Compare the iconic qualities of hieroglyphs—and as we discussed in Chapter One, we mean *iconic* in the semiotic, representation sense—with the later stages of Babylonian cuneiform (literally, "wedge-shaped") writing in Image 3.3. While both systems were used for religious purposes, *medunetjer* was much more frequently reserved for that role in Egyptian culture, whereas cuneiform texts more commonly recorded laws, medical advice, and everyday business transactions. It is unclear which writing system came first, but both represent an important transition from using pictures for *symbolic representation* to using them for *transmitting information*. Note that the other writing systems that are thought to have arisen independently in China show a similar progression from the sacred to the mundane (in Central America, symbolic representation was also a key feature of independently emerging writing systems).

All of these systems began by representing their subjects more or less directly through imagery, but were increasingly made with an abstract style over time, as that was speedier to write. Cuneiform quickly shifted from iconic characters not unlike hieroglyphs to the more familiar wedges, while hieroglyphic writing was adapted into the Phoenician alphabet, then the Greek and Etruscan, and finally the Roman. As long as the information

IMAGE 3.3 Left: Cuneiform is the ancestor of many European and Asian writing systems; **right**: the standardized shapes of Carolingian minuscule helped lead to the print forms of the Roman alphabet we see today

contained in these simplified images, whether words or sounds—or both—was being successfully transmitted, the images could become more abstract. This led to a greater focus on *legibility*, which allows readers to distinguish the differences between letters, or more precisely *graphemes*, the smallest units of written language. However, because of this pictorial heritage, literacy in its usual sense still contains an element of visual literacy. With the exception of systems like Braille, when reading printed text, ultimately we are still just looking at strings of pictures, to which we assign meanings. The correspondence between sounds and letters is more or less arbitrary—is there anything about the shape of the letter A that suggests the sound it makes?—but we tend to judge the shapes themselves for their similarity to the forms we're used to. In essence, letters have become icons of themselves.

Recognizable, standardized scripts like Carolingian minuscule (see the right side of Image 3.3) and Chinese seal script facilitated the spread of literacy before the advent of mechanical printing. Court scribes and religious workers labored to master the "proper" ways of copying a text, from the early medieval period to the Renaissance (roughly 500–1700 A.D.), and knowing the minute variations in each trained scribe's handwriting allows experts to glean more context from historical documents. Even through the print era, analyzing the *shape* of written letters, rather than what they signify, can highlight ideologies about education, tradition, and capital. As early publishers like Johannes Gutenberg and Aldus Manutius began to print writing from cast metal type (note that *font* comes from the same root as *foundry*), they maintained this diversity of writing styles and all that they implied. Over the following centuries, the number of typefaces continued to multiply at a steady rate, but once word processors became widely available and physical type was no longer necessary, typefaces enjoyed an explosive renaissance. Yet handwritten text is still valued, with calligraphy—what we might call a kind of individualized or idiosyncratic font—surviving as an art form around which whole traditions have been developed, especially in Eastern Asia and the Arabic-speaking areas.

Despite the long historical arc from highly stylized picture-writing to stylized abstraction, and the millions of possible ways we now have for representing a given stretch of script, we still have a strong response over which ones are appropriate for different situations. For example: what is your reaction between reading this font, this one, and **this one**? Which is most appropriate for this text? The division between serif and sans-serif fonts is as much about medium (is the text for the printed page or the screen?) as it is about formality. Multimodality, which we will discuss in Chapter 5, and hypertext have enriched our understanding of text formatting; an underlined word of a different color is probably a hyperlink, while hovering over an image sometimes provides more information through pop-up text. What does all of this mean for literacy? Is there a point at which all the aspects of text we deal with now can convey *too much* meaning? Time will tell, but as long as media keep changing and developing, and the forms of text become more democratized, choices about how to present text, like fonts—and our understanding of them in relation to each other—will continue to be a relevant part of the equation.

Religion, Ideology, and Representation

It's important to remember that the world does not exist in a vacuum. Everything that crosses the visual field and is assembled into something to be interpreted becomes framed by our experiences and beliefs. The term *ideology* describes a system of such beliefs, often one that is shared by a dominant social group, and that directs opinions about a wide variety of people and things without necessarily reflecting their actual qualities. A relevant example for our discussion of the evolution of visuality is *religious* ideology, which is not synonymous with faith, but instead suggests a worldview centered on (a specific) religion, the way it functions in society, and its relationship to people and the social environment. Christianity has been a primary factor influencing the history of Europe; Buddhism has done the same for many parts of Asia. As the cultures under the influence of different religions develop over time, the people in them will find their practices—including media production and consumption—shaped by and understood in relation to ideologies like these. (Note there are other kinds of ideology such as national ideologies, gender ideologies, economic ideologies and so forth—we are focusing on religion here as one instance of how ideology appears in Western culture, especially through art.)

Consider the Gothic cathedrals built in various corners of Europe between 1100 and 1500 A.D. Architects and engineers can talk about the development of building techniques that enabled higher structures and more windows, while art historians might trace the roots of decorative features in the arches or the paintings used for décor. What we are concerned with here is how a cathedral, in whole or in part, was *seen* by the people who occupied it on a daily basis. Within the religious ideology of the time, elevation was equated with being closer to God; we still see some of this metaphorical thinking at work today, when heaven is both verbally and visually positioned as being *above*. The fact that cathedrals rose far higher than any other buildings in their respective cities emphasizes the importance that the Church had as an intermediate point between God and the community. Some scholars have also suggested that the greater proportion of windows to walls stems from a similar conception, with light being linked to divinity. To the average townsperson in medieval Europe, encountering one of these buildings was to perceive, perhaps daily, a justification for (and evidence of) the prevailing ideology of religion as supreme.

On a more everyday level, different features of the cathedral also served to educate the people, and perhaps further entrench ideology. Stained glass windows served as a kind of pictorial Bible for the illiterate majority through the use of *motifs* to illustrate the stories told at Sunday Mass (see Image 3.4). Many cathedral floors feature a labyrinth design that may symbolize a religious journey, while gargoyles and grotesque three-dimensional creatures lining the stonework served as reminders of evil. Relics like the fingerbones or hair clippings of saints preserved in gold and glass displays provide a connection—some stronger than others—to moments in religious history, and statues of saints are recognizable from their dress or the objects they were portrayed with. Feast day celebrations would be an opportunity for the people (especially those named after the saint in question, for whom it was as good as a second birthday) to observe and strengthen in their memory the iconography—or, when speaking about saints, the *hagiography*—of their patron. Perhaps not

IMAGE 3.4   Christ and the Apostles, 12th century, Strasbourg Cathedral

all of these elements were intuitive, but given the unity of religious imagery, once they were internalized, a person familiar with the common patterns and themes could read the scenes in any church window, or examine the pictures in an otherwise incomprehensible book, and understand them.

Christianity does not have a monopoly on this iconographic history mixed with ideology, either. The prohibition on depicting living beings in certain traditions of Islamic art led to a focus on geometric designs, which some have retroactively read as signifying the infinite. Buddhist stupas suggest the form of the seated Buddha, while sculptures of him from different regions vary according to his appearance and the placement of his hands, with particular meanings assigned to each. What we must remember is that beyond the aesthetic qualities of any of these artworks, they served a function: to highlight religious experiences, beliefs, and duties for the onlooker. The visuality of a religious practitioner is colored by this awareness and the ideology that permeates it, just like any other system that relies upon seeing the world around us. By recognizing a space and objects in it as religious, a person understands what action they are supposed to take according to their culture's norms, and responds accordingly. Ideology allows the visual world to have a direct impact on our behavior, through which it perpetuates itself.

The Invention of Perspective

While the artists of the European Renaissance, in particular Brunelleschi (born 1377, died 1446), are often credited with "discovering" perspective, in truth there had already been many attempts to accurately represent depth on a flat surface. You might think otherwise by looking at earlier paintings, where people are the size of the buildings they're trying to enter, and whole cities are crammed into tiny portions of the panel (see the top panel of Image 3.5). Early experiments in perspective had to contend with a long history of representing and arranging subjects in accordance with their symbolic importance rather than their actual size or shape, as well as—in Europe at least— the medieval period when ancient classical knowledge about geometry, and by extension optics, was partly lost within the culture. Whether the acceleration of understanding of how vision works (as we dealt with in Chapter 2) inspired the desire for more realistic art, or vice versa, the growing use of perspective in the Renaissance was an important step in the evolution of European two-dimensional art. Thematic unity followed geometric unity, so that the viewers understood a painting as a single scene, meant to represent a more concrete or naturalistic reality.

IMAGE 3.5 Top: Illustration depicting the Burgundian Wars, the Battle of Nancy, from 1524; **bottom:** Giorgio Vasari's (1511–1574) fresco version of the Battle of Marciano; notice how the use of perspective is much more developed in Vasari's work

Other methods that define art of the period include *sfumato* (Italian for *evaporating like smoke*), a soft blending of colors that masks lines and discrete shapes, and *chiaroscuro* (Italian for *light-dark*), the contrasting use of light and darkness to create the appearance of depth. Artworks such as da Vinci's *Mona Lisa* and the portraits of Caravaggio and Rembrandt exemplify these techniques (see also Image 4.3 for a contemporary example). The overall impression is one of realism heightened to the point of optical illusion, reaching its peak in the fashion for *trompe l'œil* (French for *trick the eye*) paintings in the Baroque period

(c. 1600–1750). Again, these techniques were not unknown to previous eras, but their popularity speaks to an ideological shift; how did realism develop, supplanting in part the symbolic representation of earlier eras?

Over the same time span (roughly 1300–1600), the ideology of *humanism* was developing across Europe, borrowing from rediscovered classical literature an emphasis on a rational understanding of the world, a world to be seen and interpreted from a human point of view. Perspective, subjects with recognizable individuality, and a sense of "being there" begin to emerge as dominant ways of making visual meaning. Note that a focus on realistic depictions did not require realistic subjects. For example, the iconography and appearance of Greek and Roman deities and mythological creatures were given realistic forms, even if their viewers did not believe they existed. Each of these figures was widely recognizable to an educated audience from their iconography, just as the saints or Gospel narratives were.

Obviously, the influence of religion did not vanish, and the Church appropriated many of the new artistic techniques and concepts to further enrich its own visual language. Biblical figures such as Moses or David were presented in a manner suggesting ancient Greek sculpture, while some of the most dazzling examples of perspective can be found on the ceilings of churches. But despite the renewed interest in science drawn from classical and pagan sources and the artistic impulses it informed, the more significant shift was in the conventions of what art "should" look like. The primacy of accurately depicting reality, which can even be seen in the terms "image" and "imagine" derived from the old French and related to the notion of creating a direct likeness of something, has lasted into our own times. Visual literacy often features an evaluative component; when we ask whether what we're looking at is any *good,* we are often asking whether it conforms to our sense of realistic representation. (We also might want it to push the boundaries of what we expect in an interesting way.) This examination of form and execution, and the hierarchy of what makes some works good and others bad, became as much a part of reading art as is the consideration of the content. Again, this is an ideological concern that is neither required nor permanent, as we can see from both the fact that European art re-embraced the abstract in a number of later movements, and that not all artistic traditions around the world followed the same trajectory. But regardless of the exact rules, these issues form a key part of any past or present culture's sense of aesthetics, and by extension, their system of visuality.

ANIME AND TRADITIONAL VISUALITY IN JAPAN

Anime and manga are terms related to animated cinema and comic art produced and consumed in Japan, but with worldwide scope. As hallmarks of youth culture, most major cities in the world have a specialty shop or two that sells anime products, figurines, games, and manga. To non-fans, anime might seem to be merely Japanese "cartoons"— something that is for light amusement or satire, featuring distinct drawing styles. It may also seem very much removed from the history of Japanese art and theatre, simply because of the lack of realism in its forms of representation. Likewise, it can be associated with technologically determined kinds of art, especially when studios in Japan and subcontractors elsewhere produce anime film entirely digitally.

But aesthetically, manga and anime can be regarded as high art forms, reflecting much about traditional forms of visual storytelling in Japan and elsewhere. By relying on the relative freedom of the medium, these works can create fantastic, even magical, storylines that call heroes into being. Along with their deft handling of magic as a central element of narrative genesis, they also have traditional literary structures that play out crises and complicating actions, evoking forms of community consciousness with characters and storylines that are deeply satisfying to audiences. Both "mature" works in the genre and those aimed at younger audiences are frequently used to address tensions and paradoxes of gender (such as in the series *Ranma ½* or the 2016 film *Your Name.*), generation and tradition, politics and history (especially with films like *Barefoot Gen* that confront the horrors of war), and Japanese cultural ideologies of individual responsibility and self-expression, weighed against the needs and demands of family and society.

Many anime draw heavily on traditional Japanese art forms, often borrowing combinations of stock characters, storylines and aesthetics from novels, poetry, theatre, and visual arts. For example, calligraphy figures into many anime, sometimes being a central part of a magical narrative, and characters, landscapes, and backgrounds often show traces of visual forms like scenic scrolls that portray Japanese traditional stories, rural and urban life, and historical events (including the rise of the samurai system). In particular, anime often draws on both Noh and Kabuki theatre traditions where exaggerated make up, elaborate wigs, costumes, movement, and acting styles have long had a carefully constructed, abstracted quality that is a hallmark of Japanese aesthetics. Not only do these forms of portraying bodies, interiors, clothing, and movement (such as in fight scenes) appear in anime, projecting re-representations of traditional Japanese art to both the youth of Japan and the wider world, but anime itself has started to return to Japanese theatre. For example, in 2019, Kyoto's Minani-za Kabuki Theater created a new kabuki production based on Masashi Kishimoto's manga about a young ninja.

In a way, anime and manga remediate these older art forms, and have in turn been remediated by their export around the world, becoming an alternative to other line-drawing aesthetics that fans have grown up immersed in. For many, they are an inlet to learning about Japanese language and culture. By broadening their visual repertoire, fans expand upon and blur their definition of what visual narratives like comics and cartoons are, and what they can do.

Class and Colonialism in Modern Art

It is worth pointing out the role of *class* in both the production and distribution of art, and consequently the impact it has on culture. Throughout most of history, to become a professional artist has required a combination of talent, the time necessary to develop technical skill, and either independent wealth or the support of a guild or a patron. On the one hand, this relationship could really limit what artists were allowed to explore. Consider how medieval Church leaders would want to restrict subject matter, or how politics and intrigue might lead to the artists of one court being favored over another. But on the other hand, artists' innovations often entered the visual lexicon and gained legitimacy through the commissions and collections of the rich and powerful. Pierre Bourdieu's work *Distinction* famously discusses the link between *financial* and **cultural capital**, implying that artwork the upper classes patronize—whether the results are what they expected or not—becomes a marker of "good taste." Thus, cultural capital is the idea that intangible qualities around the attractiveness of style and form have their own special worth. Through the development of cultural capital, *fine art*, with its continuous evolution of new techniques, becomes separated from the *folk art* of the common people.

Class and social structure, however, are tangled up with *ideology*, which can be defined as a set of core ideas of economy and power that are directly related peoples' beliefs. As a society's ideologies shift over time, so will its cultural output. From the Renaissance with its emphasis on humanism, through the Enlightenment era of the 18th century and its faith in the individual, to the growing nationalist sentiments of the 19th and early 20th centuries, the old boundaries of ruling and lower classes blurred, and with that the ideas of what art should contain. New groups of painters began to practice their craft to satisfy themselves, as summed up by Caspar David Friedrich, a German Romanticist painter: "the artist's feeling is his law." (Note the gendered element of this utterance, which is equally significant in this historical aside.) Although their ideas were seen as radical at first, when artists like Degas, Monet, and van Gogh began focusing on creating atmosphere and emotion rather than precision, they appealed to the general public rather than the traditionalists. Again, this is highly localized to a Western/European context, as techniques used elsewhere in the world varied widely. For example, the tradition of ink wash painting in China was the pinnacle of refinement for centuries, equally bound up with class issues, but based on a different hierarchy of values than Europe's fixation on "accuracy."

Class is a factor in how we see the world itself, too: how do you think a millionaire and a person in poverty look at a city street differently when they walk down it? Suddenly, art reflected more of how the lower and middle classes might see things, as cheaper supplies and cheaper means of distribution meant more artists could rise from those sectors of society and have their work appreciated by greater numbers of people. Furthermore, the 19th century saw the globe becoming more interconnected through trade and technology, allowing artists to become exposed to foreign techniques that further complicated the idea of what constituted "proper" art. It's not that European art hadn't experienced diversity before, but always with the underlying sense of the long-standing social and cultural values that drove its production. Now, it was becoming democratized and individualized, put into the hands of the common people with less of the baggage of previous centuries, enabling them to appropriate more and more content from elsewhere.

Besides the social class of audiences as influence, the cultural origins of art also became an important selling point. One well-known case is the *Japonisme* movement, a fascination with all things Japanese that arose in the late 1800s, when the closed society of Japan began to reopen trade with the West. Whether or not you recognize the *Great Wave* image below (see Image 3.6), if you are a Western reader, chances are you've been acculturated into thinking of this as the Japanese drawing style. These prints, called 浮世絵 (*ukiyo-e*), were interpreted by the European elites as the centerpiece of an exotic artistic tradition, a perception that still exists to this day. As the second major era of colonialism unfolded (roughly 1880–1960), other cultures around the world also became subject to this same process of **Orientalism**, in which the non-Western "Other" is seen as strange, alluring,

IMAGE 3.6 Hokusai, 神奈川沖浪裏 (*The Great Wave off Kanagawa*)

dangerous, and inscrutable. Artists from Gauguin to Picasso interpreted the world through this ideological lens, while their more political countrymen tried to claim and control it.

A full treatment of class and colonialism is beyond our scope here, but we do feel it is important to highlight the impact of these forces on the visual culture of the times. Whether it is art that makes upper-class taste or vice versa, the ways of seeing under different centers of power and unfamiliar ideologies often create a disconnect between the context from which art arises, and the context into which it is placed. Those *ukiyo-e* prints, for example, were mass-produced from woodblocks and used as wrapping and shipping paper by the Japanese—hardly a use that most Europeans would consider prestigious. It simply goes to show how dramatically an object can be re-interpreted from context to another.

As for what constitutes art itself, Walter Benjamin's classic essay *The Work of Art in the Age of Mechanical Reproduction* (1936) discusses the concept of "authenticity" in visual media. He argues that although art has always been reproducible, the ability to do so mechanically, at much greater scale, has altered it both in terms of presence (visual media can be found almost everywhere) and nature (the definition of art becomes much broader). We can extend this argument further to say that the dynamics of power have equally altered those two aspects: various ways of seeing have been carried around the world, but often layered with new and different meaning.

And of course, the 19th century was also when experiments in photography began; as this new medium became more closely tied to an ideology of accuracy, painting as a unique and physically active form returned in part to its roots in the aesthetics of *experience*. Remember that it is in a large part *through media* that we learn our ways of seeing. The irony—or perhaps the tragedy—is that painting hasn't seemed to totally shake a veneer of the propriety that used to be its hallmark. Our culture has by and large embraced photography and realism as its preference, while much of painting is relegated once again to the realm of the elite. We must bear this in mind as we think about our ecosystem of media circulating around each other, all different systems of visuality in conversation with each other and with other aspects of culture, to be navigated and understood.

Exercises

1. Ancient Egyptian artists strove to follow the conventions of the art of their times, and although they were relatively high-status people, they did not promote their individuality through distinctive art forms or markings like signature or personal symbols embedded in art. By contrast, European painters were often signing their paintings by the 18th century, and the notion that an artist is a unique, creative individual with a specific style became widespread. What kinds of visual work in contemporary culture do *not* highlight the individual creator? In other words, what kinds of art are anonymous or at least, do not directly acknowledge the individual who created it? Come up with some examples of both signed and unsigned artwork, highlighting their creator and ignoring their creator's individuality. Does anonymous art nonetheless celebrate or promote individual creators? How do anonymous forms contrast with forms that celebrate individualized work? Why do these differences occur and what might they mean?

2. If you were to make a series of illustrated scenes and stained glass windows for an illiterate audience, what would you do? Think about the kind of information you want to convey (not necessarily religious), and who your audience would be. What famous figures, historical moments, places, and objects could you depict? Describe how you would design your work, and what elements would be recognizable enough to the viewers that they would understand your intention.

3. Even the smallest elements of a writing system can convey meaning. A serif font on a heavy metal T-shirt, full of little flairs and overhangs on its letters, suggests something quite

different from a slick san serif font announcing the name of a law firm in a skyscraper lobby. Spend a day collecting information on the fonts you see around you. Make notes or take snapshots wherever you encounter text that catches your eye: signs in your apartment building or home, on packaging, in books, on internet websites, in stores, on titles on television, etc. In each case, take note of the writing's features: is it handwritten or typed? What kind of font is being used (and is it serif or sans serif)? How do people use bold or underline or italics or color, and is there a discernible pattern in their use? Think about what impact the letters (or other graphemes) of each text have on you, and why you think the writers in each case might have chosen the font (or other aspects) they did.

For Further Exploration

Berger, John. (1990) (originally 1972). *Ways of Seeing*. New York, NY: Penguin Books.

- Seminal work on how we see culture as a visual phenomenon: "we explain the world with words, but words can never undo the fact that we are surrounded by it."

Curtis, Gregory. (2006). *The Cave Painters: Probing the Mysteries of the World's First Artists*. New York, NY: Knopf.

- "A cave painting history for everyone."

King, Ross. (2013). *Brunelleschi's Dome: How a Renaissance Genius Reinvented Architecture*. New York, NY: Bloomsbury Publishing.

- Colorful, highly readable biography of the Florentine architect who engineered the great dome of the Cathedral at Florence. Brunelleschi changed how we see perspective and the science of civil engineering.

4

PHOTOGRAPHY, FILM, AND VISUAL STORYTELLING

Introduction

We have already alluded to the historical tension in Western Art between representations growing more "realistic" and more "abstract." To some extent, an artist's medium restricts their options for representation: a mosaic can only show so much detail, and charcoal is limited to grayscale depictions of color. Clearly, there is also a relationship between media and the historical/cultural moment in which they appear and catch on (think of the eras of the telegraph, radio, digital music…), but it's not always easy to tell how the medium influences the culture, or vice versa. Does the invention of a medium lead people to develop and then demand its possibilities, or do the demands of people lead to those inventions in the first place?

While this chicken–or–egg question cannot be easily resolved, we argue that regardless of how new media and their cultures unfold, the case of photography led to a particular *paradigm shift* in how we think about visual representation. Thomas Kuhn coined this term in his book *The Structure of Scientific Revolutions* to refer to moments in scientific history where whole disciplines have been re-formulated because of a change in their most basic principles. Think, for example, of what medicine was like before bacteria were discovered, or physics before Galileo, Kepler, and Newton. But scientific disciplines are not the only thing that can be dramatically altered in this way. Photography upended the idea of what representation could be, introducing an astonishing level of detail independent of an artist's manual skill and dexterity. Film similarly changed the ideals of representation, and arguably the Internet has recently done the same.

This chapter focuses on how evolving ideals and ways of visual representation ultimately affect how we regard our social worlds and ourselves. It is useful to talk about the **epistemology** of representation, where epistemology refers to the theory of how knowledge is generated. What is it that we "know" about representation? Why do we believe there is such a thing as *accuracy* and realism in representation, while by contrast, religious icon painters and sculptors maintain the notion that *symbolism* reflects true knowledge? Why do some artists found, create, or express underlying truths of experience through *abstraction*? Of course, there are occasions when the symbolic is more directly utilitarian than the accurate, such as stylized subway maps, and the abstract may have emotional impact, such as in a Rothko painting or in the geometries of traditional Islamic gardens. Our knowledge system allows for these different cases. Still, accuracy is a value that has catapulted into more or less the top spot; as photography has grown more prevalent, more accessible, it has come to seem more *real* to us than other visual media.

The Rise of Photography

It is no accident that photography appeared during the preoccupation with natural science and documentation in the Enlightenment era; appropriately, the word *photography* itself means "light writing." Artists had already long used the phenomenon of the *camera obscura*, wherein light shining through a small hole will project an image (albeit upside down) onto the wall of a room, or a mirror, or a box, as a guide to trace buildings or landscapes. But they did not have a way to create durable and mechanically reproducible impressions of these images until the byproducts of early chemistry experiments revealed more and more substances that darkened when exposed to light. Through the chemistry of photography, the theoretical possibility of recording a direct image of something slowly became a reality. Pioneering work by Frenchmen Nicéphore Niépce and Louis Daguerre in the 1820s and 1830s caused a sensational boom in interest in photographs and the budding science of photography, and soon dozens of inventors were creating (and patenting) their own processes, devices, and combinations of materials in search of the perfect photo.

What was it about photography that so quickly captured the public consciousness? Certainly it put the upper-class phenomenon of the portrait within reach of the growing middle class, and allowed them to take on some of that cultural prestige. Photographers also did not have to spend as long learning their trade as painters, with a result that might be more accurate in terms of portraying the look of something directly, for better or for worse, than a painter could achieve. Think of how many common elements of modern life would be different without photos: birth announcements, identity cards, front-page newspaper articles, travel guides, etc. When we talk about early photography, we often focus on how sitters could not smile because of the long exposure times required, the lack of color, or the poorer overall quality of the image. Yet for many of these sitters, this would be the only permanent record they had of how they had looked, a treasure that's easy to dismiss in the era of the daily selfie.

Speaking of newspapers, journalism was quick to take up the new practice. The Crimean War and American Civil War are often discussed as the first conflicts whose battlefields and soldiers were photographed by journalists, giving civilians a

IMAGE 4.1 Alexander Gardner, Antietam dead gathered for burial during the American Civil War, 1862

dramatic sense of events taking place far away (see Image 4.1). Previously, an artist's subjective views could literally be painted into the scene, where the stroke of the brush edited the "reality" of the subject—perhaps to make them look taller or smarter, or to place them in a country landscape, or to paint a beautiful gown on them. These creative choices were an inherent part of the work. With photography, creating a compelling work requires different kinds of effort, and the choice of what object to photograph or the angle at which to approach a photographic subject becomes a more pivotal part of the creative process.

It is no coincidence that because of the more reliable and realistic qualities of its portrayal, photography began to affect human inquiry about science. ("Reliable" here refers to how likely multiple photos of the same subject will resemble each other, and the person they are trying to portray; multiple oil portraits of the same subject are less reliable, meaning they are not always going to have a notable or quite as exact resemblance to the subject or to each other.) As a new technology, photography was explored by people like Harold Edgerton, an engineer at the Massachusetts Institute of Technology who photographed events at extremely high speeds, such as balloons popping and bullets firing. These photos are interesting for their apparent "realism" in that they can show us events that the human eye cannot normally see. They are also invaluable for scientists who seek to understand these physical processes. But how realistic is photography, and why do we buy into its realism when we cannot actually do with our own vision what photography does? Does it show us forms of reality that we do not experience with the naked eye, or, remembering persistence of vision, does it simply give us greater insight into what we do see? Consider how the paradigm of what is considered *real* can change from something as simple as a photographic series that lets us see for the first time how a human or a horse runs (see Image 4.2). And this evolution is far from over; when did we come to see special

IMAGE 4.2 Eadweard Muybridge experimented with photography in the late 1870s to capture the movements of people and animals. His video loop of a horse galloping was an overnight sensation, and his films went on a sold out tour of the United States and Europe.

effects work in film photography as enhancing the "realism" of a spaceship or a ghoul from another dimension?

As photography became the norm for family and individual portraits, and as it was eventually used for illustrations and artwork in magazines and newspapers, photography became appreciated for its own unique aesthetic potential. The effects of lighting and shadow reflected the Italian Renaissance principle of *chiaroscuro*, and as photographic techniques improved, artists made full use of the new cameras to create dramatic portraits, as in Image 4.3. The possibilities grew significantly once color

IMAGE 4.3 Film star Marlene Dietrich, in a still photo by Don English from the Paramount Pictures film Shanghai Express (1932); studio production experts quickly learned how to manipulate lighting in film and photography to harness the drama of *chiaroscuro* principles in photographic media

IMAGE 4.4 Sergey Prokudin-Gorsky's photo of Staraya Ladoga church, 1909; the photos were taken through red, green, and blue filters, which could be projected or printed using all three at once to create a full-color result

photography became workable enough, and certainly affordable enough, to be common by the 1950s and 1960s. But there are some pieces from the adolescence of photography whose quality is astonishing for their time. Consider the work of Sergey Prokudin-Gorsky (see Image 4.4), who built a mobile photographic studio in the early 1900s to travel around the Russian Empire, documenting the lives of its peoples, its architecture, and its landscapes. Even before their retouching by the Library of Congress, his prints are remarkable for their clarity and color, thanks to his method of using different filters to quickly capture three images in a row of the same subject. (You can see remnants of the filters on the edges of the photo, indicating that the process used to produce it in color is probably different from the higher-tech versions that you're used to.)

We want to return to the question of how many early photos were "true to life." Realism is always just an idea, not a one-to-one representation of what is "real" in the world. Accuracy does not always entail *authenticity*, a characteristic that is troublesome to define. To put it another way, an image can be as detailed as possible and still show something that does not reflect reality, depending on how it is presented and the context in which it is created. We have already discussed the importance of being self-aware and reflexive in your own visual analyses. This emphasis on recognizing one's own position grew in part as a reaction to early anthropologists' tendency to stage some of the "native scenes" they were documenting, and the desire of later anthropologists and cultural critics to ask: how do our expectations about realism, accuracy and authenticity affect our ways of seeing? Moreover, the style of realism is often deployed in propaganda, where film and photography had a lot to do with the rise of dictatorships and widespread espionage in the early 20th century. Photographs are often meant to be impartial reminders of historical moments, but it should also be noted that many have been edited after the fact when the history they depict becomes problematic for the state. A worrisome trend in recent decades has been the inherent distrust of photographs which do not support the onlooker's worldview, and outright creation of ones that do, taking the break between accuracy and authenticity to its extreme. These themes are explored in detail in Chapter 7.

Film and Its Codes

For centuries, people experimented with illusions of moving images, from shadow puppets to zoetropes (photographs in a rotating cylinder that when spun, show a loop of animated movement). But with the technology of photography becoming widespread and developing rapidly, it was only a matter of time before late 19th century inventors made the leap to film. Modern film really began with the creation of stable film stock that could be run through a single camera in real time, rather than taking a series of photographs and displaying them more quickly than the eye could follow. As with early photography, many inventors tried to perfect the process, such as Louis LePrince (widely recognized as the first to successfully "shoot" a film), the workshop of Thomas Edison, and the Lumière brothers in France. The early cameras had to take pictures rapidly enough that they would trigger the eye's *motion perception,* a rate at which individual images follow upon each other enough that the eye cannot perceive the boundaries between them. Early films often look jerky and unrealistic because their *frame rate* was on the low boundary of motion perception, around 12–24 frames per second, or they may have been poorly calibrated in projection and shown too slowly. As technology improved, the look of films became smoother and smoother and today many feature length movies are recorded and screened at speeds of up to 72 frames per second.

Almost from the moment of its invention, film was used for narrative purposes. When the viewer tries to move outside the instant captured by a photograph, they are necessarily making assumptions about the past and future of the subject. By contrast, films remove some of this burden from the viewer, leading them from one scene to the next. Marshall McLuhan referred to films as a "hot" medium, one that engages our senses (certainly the visual and the emotional) totally and does not require the viewer to fill in details. A popular myth is that at one of the earliest public screenings in 1896, for Louis Lumière's film *Arrival of a Train at La Ciotat*, attendees were frightened by the experience of a life-size train rushing at them from the screen. (Talk about audience involvement! See Chapter 6 on the concept of *hypermediacy*). With that level of engagement, filmmakers could create narratives, documentaries or fictional stories that would totally immerse their audiences, so long as the medium remained fresh and innovative, and the viewers were unused to the spectacle of moving pictures. By the early 1900s, features like Georges Méliès' *Le Voyage dans la Lune* and Edwin Porter's *The Great Train Robbery* demonstrated the potential for longer stories to captivate their audiences.

PRESERVING FILM AND VIDEO AS NATIONAL CULTURAL HISTORY AND WORLD HERITAGE

Prior to video tape and digital cameras, films were made with celluloid film stock—essentially, strips of plastic with a thin coating of gelatin in which photosensitive silver and other chemicals were embedded. All three recording processes not only create very different looking images, but they also disintegrate or degrade in different ways. Celluloid film starts to react with moisture in the air and gives off a form of vinegar that ultimately destroys it; old films not kept cool in low humidity storage do not hold up well, if at all. Sadly, only about 25% of the nearly 11,000 silent films made for cinematic distribution in the United States have survived in some form. It's even worse in India, where only five cinematic movies have survived out of about 1,700 made in the silent era. Likewise, video tape can lose magnetism and the tape itself can stretch out or become brittle. You may have family videos of yourself or your parents' generation where the tapes have degraded too badly to watch, and many "classic" 1970s and 1980s television shows worldwide have been lost to "wiping" as when the master tape are re-used by studios without giving a thought to archives. Finally, digital images are theoretically able to last forever, but maintaining them is complicated by technological issues including: changes in video and audio quality due to different kinds of compression for different formats; potential loss of titles and subtitles; and certain effects because of how the programming of a new storage format "reads" the moving images in question.

Recognizing that moving images are an important part of our cultural history, private individuals, foundations, and governments all over the world have helped to establish film preservation and restoration groups. For example, in 1996, the United States Library of Congress, in conjunction with the Academy of Motion Picture Arts and Sciences (yes, the people who give out Oscars), created the National Film Preservation Foundation, dedicated to identifying films unlikely to survive. The foundation works to coordinate photo labs and film archives to figure out how to preserve and sometimes restore items, although film and video continue to disintegrate faster than they can be saved; often the images need to be transferred to a longer-lasting medium. Archivists seek out American documentaries, silent films, newsreels, historically important home movies, avant-garde works, industrial films and independent works to preserve, although they also do sometimes work internationally to preserve major release films.

In the last decade, much of film preservation has also gone international, and most nations have groups that work together to save moving images as part of our world heritage. The Film Heritage Foundation of India, which has a similar mission to the US National Film Preservation Foundation, works internationally to train Indian filmmakers and archivists to preserve audio and video works. They also do regional film preservation work, reflecting India's multiple centers for cinema production in various languages, including Telugu and Bengali.

Part of what differentiated film from theater—the other main medium of visual narrative as a public spectacle—was the development of cinematic semiosis through editing techniques. Consider the differences between two photos placed side by side in a gallery, and a cut from one scene to another in a film. While the photos do not necessarily have an interrelationship that you are meant to divine (however, see the section on graphic novels below), a filmic cut or edit carries recognizable meaning, either to illustrate a plot connection between two or more shots that make up a scene or a sequence, or to remind the audience that there are multiple characters and subplots to keep track of. Scenes that fade to black might show us the passage of time, while scenes that cut directly to another shot within the same scene show sequence of events. Or consider the long shot of a landscape: how does a stationary photo differ from a film shot that slowly pans across the landscape, zooms in to focus on something specific, or that allows the filmmaker to show changes in time with sunrises, sunsets, and clouds rolling in?

Early films quickly conventionalized these techniques and they spread widely until most viewers were able to recognize their meanings, solidifying them as filmic *codes* that directors could obey, expand upon, or flout. Just like photographers, filmmakers slowly built upon these standardized codes to create individual styles, and eventually film aesthetics. Directors like Fritz Lang, D.W. Griffith, and Sergei Eisenstein are often described as early pioneers in pushing the boundaries of the new codes to create cinematic art. For more specific information on filmic codes, see the special section called *Narrative Conventions in Film—Key Examples* at the end of this chapter.

And as with photography, the types of narratives that can be conveyed are many. Film was taken up as a narrative tool by journalists for recording newsworthy events, by scientists to document processes in real time, and by artists to expand the narrative potential of theater by the use of special effects. Of course, with such an influential medium, it did not take long for governments to adapt film to their own purposes, creating widespread propaganda before and during World War II. This calls attention to another important aspect of narrative, or texts in general: what Saussure called the *syntagmatic* and *paradigmatic* dimensions. The first is concerned with the ordering of signs to create a meaningful narrative, since a sign can only possess so much meaning when it stands in isolation. Think of it as how we put together meanings out of *sequences* of words or images. The paradigmatic axis, meanwhile, deals with the many options that a sign producer has when deciding what should come next in the sequence of signs. Each step in a narrative can be followed by a number of others, and the option that the writer/photographer/director chooses is as significant as what they do *not* choose. For propaganda, this is especially clear: by definition, this genre selectively includes and excludes certain information in order to provoke a specific response in the viewer, especially if giving them more complete information would create a more neutral response. On the one hand, for any narrative that is not wholly fictional, it is basically impossible to include *everything* that could be said; on the other, what is included often exposes the creator's own biases and subjectivity.

As technology has continued to develop, filmmakers have introduced sound, color, special effects, 3-D and various experiments with virtual reality to the world of cinema. The rise of CGI (*computer generated imagery*) has allowed the creation of entire characters and worlds outside of our material world. But the flipside to the ever-improving techniques of image manipulation is that old question: how can we trust what we see? What do we accept, and what do we question?

On Television

There has been extensive work done on television, its history, its differences with film, and much more. But for our purposes here, it's enough to point out how some of its basic qualities as a medium, both mechanical and social/cultural, differ from film. The two have more in common in terms of visuality than not, sharing much of the same visual language and similar narrative genres.

Most readers, if not all, will be intimately familiar with some form(s) of television broadcast. When the TV first arrived on the scene in the mid-20th century, it quickly became a marker of middle-class success, transforming the living room into a theatrical space that could be enjoyed privately by the family. (Movie theaters, desperate to make up the cut to their business, became more willing to show edgier films that would not pass television network censors, leading to cinema being seen as a more mature, artsy medium.) Over time, television has been delivered by traditional airwaves received on an aerial antenna on the roof, through a cable hardwired to come into the home, as recordings to be played through a playback device, and through internet-based content delivery on a smart television or related device. Now, many of us watch television that is played on computers and hand held devices, even smart phones. It might even make more sense to refer to contemporary television as "streaming content" given the dominance of internet services, podcasts, and timed broadcasts on cable TV (often recorded on a digital video recorder, aka DVR), all playable on various devices.

All of this makes watching television feel much more *à la carte* than it used to. Note that until recently, television was seen as a "democratized" medium; besides the fact that most families in many countries had one, stations chose what could be seen at a given time by everybody with a TV. The wider range of technology that can receive moving images of this type means that the patterns of production, distribution, and consumption have changed too—which is as important to understand about the evolution of television as the characteristics of its content. As a medium, television obviously has continuity with filmmaking, but for a long time, it was normally either live (as in news broadcasts) or episodic (as in serial show content, usually very formulaic), rather than a standalone narrative. Likewise, television shows (and some online services) are often subject to paid advertising segments, another form of unique visual production.

Contemporary television actually differs less from cinematic film than did the television of the 1950s through the 1990s. Today, the dividing line between "movie stars" and "television stars" is blurred to the point it almost doesn't exist. Likewise, instead of advertisers paying for the cost of television production, many individuals now pay for streaming content only. A lot of this content (what is sometimes called "prestige TV") has higher production values than the videotaped in-studio television of the past, often with episodes longer than television from previous decades, allowing for bigger casts and more supporting scenes. (The name of the groundbreaking content creator HBO, "Home Box Office," shows this alignment with cinema pretty directly.). Our home entertainment systems as well make watching television and movies a much more cinematic experience than it was in the past.

Additionally, with greater budgets for cinematic television, the narrative style of contemporary television has changed to include more location shots and shows shot entirely on location, more historical settings with elaborate (for television) scenes and costumes, and special effects. At the same time, however, shows on television remain less oriented toward visual experimentation than in movie-theater cinema; "art theaters" are still open and serving movie going audiences, while the biggest blockbusters try to draw people into the cinema on both super-star power and the idea of a unique experience, for example, by featuring more food and drink options and luxury recliners. The rising cost of going to the theater also works against them; why go out to see a film when you can watch high-budget content at your leisure, on a flatscreen that may take up most of your wall, for free (or at least, free after the cost of your monthly bill)? To come back to our brief, this difference matters for visuality, too. If the stakes are higher for seeing a film (you have to pay money, you have to be punctual, you might have to drive there, etc.), the level of visual and intellectual attention and emotion involved in your attitudes towards it are probably different than they are for an episode of *Great British Bake Off* playing in the background at home. It's just one more example of how our ways of seeing are heavily tied up in these technological histories and social practices, even as the distinctions between media become less and less clear.

CHANGING FILM FORMATS: COORDINATING TECHNOLOGY

Filmmakers, movie houses, photo and production labs, commercial and consumer electronics makers, and content providers (i.e., cable and streaming video makers, as well as internet and smart phone applications) have always had to coordinate changing technology in order to bring visually appealing moving images to audiences. Sometimes special movie technologies are gimmicks. "Sensurround" was created by Cerwin-Vega (an audio company) and Universal Studios in 1974 to promote the movie *Earthquake* and featured shaking seats. Sensurround was of course complex to install and maintain, and it obviously did not catch on permanently (despite the glut of 1970s disaster movies). Another special technology of the past was Cinemascope, developed by 20th Century Fox and installed in their worldwide network of theaters as a direct response to a screen technology called Cinerama developed by a Fox Studios engineer. Both Cinerama and Cinemascope were created with an aspect ratio that privileged the horizontal frame, giving audiences a sense of immersion in the screen, as though their entire field of vision was inside the landscapes and scenes of the movies. This technology was developed and utilized by moviemakers, and it caught on widely for a while in the 1950s, even though it sometimes required costly retrofitting of screens in theaters.

With the advent of digital televisions, there are ever more options for audio and visual inputs that provide a considerable challenge to making content work everywhere with consistently high quality; this includes various formats for content distribution, various types of sound and video production, and audio and visual hardware within televisions. For example, televisions come with post-processing interfaces (computer programming as well as hardware) that include something called motion smoothing, or sometimes "sports mode." Motion smoothing was developed for digital television in the 1990s, to compensate for how fast moving images—especially baseballs and footballs—have poor quality when viewed at various digital *refresh rates*, meaning the number of times per second an image is fully reloaded across a television screen. Coordinating technologies for refresh rates, digital film production technologies, viewer tastes and habits, and the artistic intent of the original producers of the moving images is a very complicated task, and motion smoothing technologies have to be carefully coordinated across all of these platforms and stakeholders. With all that, it's rather amazing that this kind of content can be viewed at all.

Motion smoothing, however, is also called "soap opera mode" in a derogatory way because it makes computer-generated imagery, as well as movies filmed on celluloid at 24 or 72 frames per second, look "fake." You can easily find videos online that demonstrate this particular look. Big shot movie directors—who have a lot of power in the motion picture industry—have pushed successfully for new modes on our televisions, something like a "Filmmaker" or "Cinema" mode, that allows us to toggle off motion smoothing, so that we can see movies with images that more closely resemble what the directors and producers intended.

Aspects of Storytelling

Obviously, different forms of visual media will make use of different strategies to get their narrative across to an audience. But if we step back from the particulars of one form or another, we can see that certain patterns in the visual meanings embedded in narrative are present within the wider culture. One of the clearest examples is that of *gaze*, as exemplified by media theorist Laura Mulvey when she specified the *male gaze* in cinema: the phenomenon where the audience, by way of the camera, is meant to identify with a male point of view (often the protagonist's). This entails a level of objectification towards women that feminist scholars have further explored in critiques of visual media. While the viewer might not actually relate to one character or another in a film, remember the notion of paradigmatic choice: there are a number of ways that women can be framed and portrayed in the shots of a film, so why do filmmakers regularly choose the ones that show women as passive, and often eroticized? Of course, this is not unique to film, and the male gaze has arguably been around for millennia in the art world; nor is gender the only category in which gazes operate. We can talk about the *heterosexual gaze*, where characters are portrayed in terms of their gender roles as if from a "straight" point of view, a *white gaze* that displays ethnic minorities in a certain light, *middle class gaze* which erases or minimizes the perspectives of the poor, and so on. Films can make use of alternative viewpoints in each case (*female gaze*, etc.), but often this is an overt attempt to subvert the norm, where a dominant group is imposing its visual interpretations of the others.

It can sometimes be unclear whether these kinds of effects are intended by the producers of visual media, or if they are just so pervasive in our culture that they cannot help being biased. In the end, does it matter? Roland Barthes argued for what he called "the death of the author," saying that intentions are beside the point: we are inclined to assign whichever meanings we are going to whenever we look at a photo, or a film, or any other visual artifact, regardless of what the creator thinks. The complex apparatus of production ensures that everything from billboards to YouTube commercials tend to reflect one dominant visual reading (this idea is discussed extensively in Chapter 8), but there will always be other possibilities. For example, you can probably think of several incidents where a company didn't realize how many people would view their new ad campaign completely differently, or how footage of a news incident from different angles changes the way the facts of the case are interpreted. Barthes introduced a line of thinking that opened up whole new schools of criticism based upon the fact that there is more than one way to read visual media, each tied up in a complex cultural relationship. This wasn't a completely new idea when he formulated it, but we are much more likely now to take it as a given; whether people respect alternative opinions remains a point of contention.

One tool that can be used to direct the interpretations of a work is *genre*, which we might describe as a set of codes applied to a narrative, so that certain interpretations the author wants are made visible to the viewer. For example, eerie music, shadowy lighting, and close-up shots of terrified faces are directorial choices that signal "this is a horror film" to the viewer. If the viewer acknowledges that fact, and is familiar with these codes, they are unlikely to judge the work primarily on (for example) the poor romantic plot developments. Likewise, some directors, actors, lighting directors, and soundtrack composers might draw on the tools of the genre in order to critique it, which happens often with satire; other times, creators might be making mashups or hybrid genres in an effort to subvert the entire idea of genre itself.

Genre can be a slippery slope, such as when audiences overlook a certain level of objectifying women in romantic comedies; a man endlessly chasing a "difficult" woman often seems to be the point of the picture, rather than being regarded as sexual harassment. We sometimes also have a problem recognizing that genres are partially founded in specific kinds of cultural ideas, and therefore they may have a limited audience who will fully "get it." Think of your friend who doesn't like comedies, or car race-chase movies, or sci-fi movies as much as you do. It would be a monumental task to push all visual media producers towards creations that are culturally neutral enough, and balanced enough, to appeal to all viewers— not that some aren't trying. The easier task is for viewers to improve their visual literacy, to recognize the underlying patterns, and take them into account when they make an assessment of the work.

Graphic Novels as Sequential Visual Phenomenon

Before we go to the next chapter, exploring the interaction of word, image, and sound in contexts outside of film-based mass media narratives, there is another important aspect of visual storytelling that must be mentioned. Theorist and cartoonist Scott McCloud explains that in the sequential art of comics, the fact of images being juxtaposed in space forces us as viewers to seek *closure*, to reconcile our interpretation of one image, with the idea present in the next image. This is the gestalt principle again (see Chapter 2)— closure is about our desire to make sense of what we see, at least enough sense to move forward, even perhaps when there is no sense. Thus, each new item must be integrated into the sense we've made of the previous item. Reading comics is a lot of work for the reader, and when one does a lot of cognitive and emotional work in images (and maybe words), one takes the material to heart in a deep way. This is part of the power of comics (see Image 4.5). Likewise, when they are drawn images, comic book characters have a range

IMAGE 4.5 *Wizard of Id* comic strip by Mick Mastroianni and Johnny Hart

of iconic qualities, where one character might be portrayed in a realistic style and look very much like a photograph, while another might be highly stylized and even abstract. For the much less iconic images, the reader works personally to insert an idea of themselves into the character's position. So, another part of the power of comics is to project the self as an act of intense imagination.

Reading comics can be contrasted to cinema, where the work of closure is done for us with multimodal effects like sound and editing. The emotional experience of watching cinema can still be intense, but as a set of images in time, rather than space, any kind of video or film narrative can be a much more passive experience. Likewise, when we identify with a person in the cinema, we may indeed project our persona upon them, but we are possibly more likely to project them as someone we know or someone we see out there in real life. After all, most of us do not look like the extremely recognizable faces of Johnny Depp or Beyoncé. We may not project *ourselves* onto them the same way we would an abstract comic character, but that moment of recognition may draw in our knowledge about them (from magazines, news interviews, or wherever) and lead us to project *something*. Abstract images require much more direct identification work on the part of the viewer, in contrast with iconic and realistic images.

SPECIAL CHAPTER SECTION: NARRATIVE CONVENTIONS IN FILM—KEY EXAMPLES

Camera angle: the camera tends to be placed at eye level relative to the viewer. Likewise, camera movement may include panning side to side, or tracking, but it is relatively rare to see tilting up and down. How does an eye-level angle affect the experience of watching a film?

Cross-cutting: alternating cuts between two different scenes. How do we as viewers "know" that the two scenes are taking place simultaneously (also called "parallel action")?

Continuity editing: cuts between scenes that maintain the same time-space. It's important that music remain the same between each shot, for example, or lighting, or that everyone is wearing the same clothing and hairstyle or the weather is the same, or extras are in the right places, and so forth. Otherwise, what kinds of interpretations does the viewer come to?

Deep focus: often, filmmakers will make both the foreground subjects and the background subjects in focus in a long shot. The human eye cannot do this, but film technology can bring it to life for us. Do we even notice this filmic convention? What about scenes where deep focus is not used—what are the filmmaker's choices about focus trying to tell us?

Dissolve: when a shot fades out of focus and into another science, the audience will presume many different things. Fade to black might mean passage of time. It might mean a key character has passed out. Dissolves sometimes lead us to dream worlds. What other conventionalized interpretations of dissolves do we have?

Establishing shot: opens a movie, or perhaps an important scene. These tend to give the viewer the big picture and set the mood for the scope and atmosphere of much of the movie. Search online for "famous establishing shots" and watch a few. What do features do they somewhat have in common?

Jump cut: cuts occurring with the same camera angle, or almost exactly the same shot, but jumping ever so slightly forward or backward in time. How do we as viewers feel emotionally when experiencing these tiny juxtapositions? Do they make us feel differently toward the character involved?

Match cut: an edit that carries over into a totally different scene or setting, usually done through sound or a continuous action (like a car movement). Despite the change in image, through the illusion of continuous action or continuous sounds, match cuts feel extremely "natural" to us, like a daily experience. Do you ever notice match cuts?

Reverse angle: these are shots taken at 180 degree angle from the previous shot, often used in a dialogue between two or more subjects in a film to create the illusion that two people are talking to each other. They are very common, but they take a lot of film experience for camera, lighting, and actors to portray realistically.

Wipe: when the whole screen with its visual material included is wiped away to reveal another scene underneath, on top or next to it. This optical illusion continues to slightly stun audiences and is part of how cinematic film is a hot medium.

Exercises

1. Search for some of the photos of Cindy Sherman. How do her photos challenge our notions of authenticity; however, you might define it? What are the conventions of the *gaze* around women that she may be commenting on? Is there any way to see her photos as realistic? If you are working in a group, what are the various responses of group members to her photos and what do you think of the range of interpretations or responses?

2. Take another look at Image 4.5. Comic readers have to work to interpret what happens between or across each frame, a process called seeking *closure*. What kind of work do you do to "close" your reading of what is happening in the two transitions between the three frames? How does the caption at the end (which requires you to recognize that Uber is a smartphone app-based ride service) confirm, reshape or otherwise affect your initial reading? Did you have to go back and recalibrate your thoughts or did you get this from the start? How would different captions influence your interpretation? Finally, comics are often visually abstract. How are readers meant to identify with these characters' abstract qualities?

3. Watch a friend play a videogame for a few minutes. What are the visual conventions of moving from item to item or scene to scene or task to task? What is the point of view of the "camera" in witnessing the action? Does the "camera" rotate with the point of view of the player, or is the player watching a static frame? Where is "eye-level" in the various parts of the game and how can you tell where it is? How would changing any of these items change the experience and the interpretation of the game?

For Further Exploration

Jackson, Peter. (2018). *They Shall Not Grow Old* (documentary film). Warner Brothers.

- Be sure to read about how Jackson and his crew restored film footage from World War I on the French front with the cooperation of the British Imperial War Museum and the BBC. Features voice overs from British soldiers.

McCloud, Scott. (1993). *Understanding Comics: The Invisible Art.* New York, NY: William Morrow.

- The semiotics of comics … in comic book form. A fun read!

Sontag, Susan. (1973). *On Photography.* New York, NY: Farrar, Strauss and Giroux.

- Surprising set of short essays on what photography means, this book is credited with putting photography in the realm of high art.

Truffaut, François. (1983). *Hitchcock.* New York, NY: Simon and Schuster.

- A series of readable and informative conversations, with lot of illustrating film stills, between two of the very greatest filmmakers of all time.

5

WORD, IMAGE, SOUND: WHAT IS MULTIMODALITY?

Introduction

When words and images come together, people tend to privilege the written word as they try to interpret what they see. When we have visual and written material in combination, we like to put a frame around these materials on walls, on manuscripts and book pages, in stained glass, on screens, and so forth. Visual material is very often captioned, and written material often has accompanying illustrations, while most videos do not feel complete or interpretable without audio. We often call these cases where various elements are packaged together *texts*, not in the textbook sense, but in the semiotic sense of them being a meaningful unit, all of whose parts contribute to how we understand the whole. We recognize it as a unified thing that an author or authors have put before us, as a kind of request that we can "read" or interpret.

This process of interpretation of such texts is ubiquitous but also very complex. Our worlds are not really flat surfaces with words on a page or pictures with frames, but three-dimensional and noisy, involving the imagination and experience, with many layers of input to decode. This chapter further develops *multimodality* as a helpful idea for grasping what we do when we interpret complicated texts with multiple parts like word-image combinations, a person's outfit, a musical performance, or the decor and signage of a store full of people. Our goal is to show you how to think about meaning-making as a *multimodal* process: how we figure out the individual meanings of each element in an associated set of images, words, sounds, smells, spatial arrangements, human behaviors, and many other things. The further we are able to work through all the components of meaning-making in these places, texts, or objects, the more coherent our understanding will be of what we are observing.

Codes, Conventions, and Interpreting Meaning

For a very long time, scholars preferred to focus primarily on language, especially written language, over other forms of meaning-making. But this belief about privileging language stemmed from other influential figures throughout history. Religious thinkers, scribes (record keepers) and historians, lawyers and politicians all focused (and some continue to do so) on recording oration and studying written words. The pen is "mightier than the sword" in part because it is a direct form of history-making—after all, words could be recorded in written form and passed down along the generations. Additionally, even though they also create meaning in human lives, technologies and practices like painting, sculpture, building, weaving, musical performances, and so forth take enormous amounts of time and expertise, and thus were often not really understood in the same terms (or necessarily given the same value) as oral and written language. This overfocus on writing has blinded us to thinking about how other sensory channels (called *modes*, which we will discuss further down) like the visual, the aural,

IMAGE 5.1 Tourists in Rome in line to obtain *biglietti* to see the Colosseum

the spatial and haptic (sense of touch), the olfactory (sense of smell), and so forth work together as part of what we interpret on a daily basis.

Before we delve further into various modes and how they interact, it is very useful to explore conceptual ideas and vocabulary to describe our processes of interpreting anything meaningful. Imagine going to see a monument or a museum while on a tourist trip to Rome, Italy (Image 5.1). As you enter, signs in (what you logically presume are) Italian tell you where to buy *biglietti*, a word whose meaning you may or may not be able to figure out. But when you find one sign with the English equivalent, 'tickets," a meaningless word like *biglietti* might suddenly become meaningful to you, as you put together how to interpret this single word in Italian. Your interpretation may feel like it is merely a basic act of translation, but actually, your mind is making a number of judgment calls to reach a conclusion. For example, you are aware of the fact that you are standing in a big line of tourists outside of an ancient Roman monument doing what tourists conventionally do—waiting to buy tickets. Moreover, all the people in this line seem to have the intention of seeing the monument and thus the intention of purchasing tickets. You also probably know that the tourism officials for the City of Rome aren't going to let people see monuments for free when tourism is an important part of the city budget, or at least that the city needs to regulate the flow of people through its structures of cultural heritage. All these clues—*language*, *patterned movement* through space, what *behaviors* others are engaging in and the *intentions* you can assume they have, knowledge about the wider *political* or *economic* or *cultural* issues that affect human behavior—help you try to interpret what is going on.

Another possibility: instead of finding an English sign, you might ask someone in line with you who "looks English" if they believe they are in the right line for buying tickets. This idea of how someone or something looks is another act of interpretation that is part of the wider experience—listening for sounds of an accent, or knowing ahead of time that British tourists are more likely to be wearing Manchester United shirts, or that American tourists are more likely to be wearing Red Sox baseball caps and Nikes, than tourists from, say, Germany or France. In these examples, you base your judgments on forms of knowledge about the norms of casual dress in at least a few nations. You make *inferences* based on the *visual* and *aural cues* around you to figure out if you can address someone in English without causing a cross-cultural misunderstanding. In visual studies terminology, these pieces put together constitute a **look**, as in the "look of an American tourist," or the "look of an entrance to a large monument."

In situations like these, especially when your interpretation or deduction might be necessary to behave properly as a tourist, there are three different elements we want to specify here. The first is the semiotic **sign**, which we've already discussed (see Chapter 1 for review). Remember that signs do not necessarily *have* to be flat objects on a pole or a storefront, though such objects are included in our definition. Think of a sign more broadly as anything, *physical or abstract*, that communicates meaning to people; in our example above, this includes the written text, but also all of the configurations of people and objects that help you refine your read of the situation. A sign does not have to be small, or static, and can sometimes be divided into parts that are each as significant as the whole. It can also mean different things to different people. The Colosseum as a sign—and a big sign it is—carries a variety of historical, religious, and national meanings, to tourists and to visitors alike. A line at a ticket booth is a sign that communicates orderly waiting, but there is a big difference between seeing or thinking about lines, and actually standing at the beginning or the end of one.

A series of signs that come together in a *regular pattern* is called a **convention**. Conventions are common practices—so common, in fact, that we experience them as accepted kinds of behavior and tend not to question them; they are seemingly subconscious. Why would a tourist question the whole idea of standing in line to see a Roman monument? After all, that is what tourists in Rome *do*. Conventions are learned through various means, but especially by experience and watching others. They are also wholly necessary to the daily function of human lives in society; having conventions for talking, driving, dressing, walking down the street, getting on and off buses, buying things, and so forth allows us to function socially and individually. Those who defy everyday conventions generally do not fare well or may end up causing trouble. (How do people in line usually react to somebody who blatantly cuts in front of them, or leaves big spaces or gaps between them and others?) Conventions also provide us mental shortcuts for getting to the more interesting things in life, like actually seeing and learning about the Roman Colosseum.

Finally, the unwritten rules for conventions are called **codes**. You can think of codes almost as laws for how to do conventions correctly, or the rules that govern how to properly use a set of conventions. Codes can also be understood as part of the local social contract. Thus, if you see signs that include a line of tourists, a physical monument, and signage advertising tickets, all coming together to suggest the convention of "waiting in line to enter a monument," then the codes might be: you must go to the end of the line, you must make sure you can pay the entry fee, you avoid talking too loudly in line, etc. Some of these are highly variable based on culture and personality, of course; how close will you stand to the person in front of you? Violating codes just a little bit can sometimes be stimulating or thought-provoking because it shakes us out of our complacency for a minute and forces us to think harder to figure out what is going on. But when someone throws out *all* the rules and completely defies the orderliness of codes and conventions, the end result may be so unconventional as to be uninterpretable.

When traveling in a foreign country, we may not know the logic behind how conventions come together in culturally specific patterns—what we might specify as *cultural codes*. These codes, concerning how to operate locally or among a specific group, govern or proscribe conventions for moving about, interpreting images, what to eat in restaurants and in what order, how to address wait staff, and other kinds of day-to-day basics. (Have you ever tried to order a cappuccino in the afternoon in Italy? Better not to!) The things going on around us often look like "chaos" at first, or perhaps appear invisible without rules or codes for behavior, yet they are there. It just takes a bit of experience and adjustment to learn what to do, and why. To sum up, codes and conventions are easily confused, but if you think of conventions as patterns, and codes as rules, you'll see the subtle differences and be able to use the terms when you need that level of detailed analysis.

The Natural(ized) Experience of Multimodality

People have to do a lot of cognitive work when they first learn to recognize individual signs, and then the conventions and codes around those signs. Think of learning to understand illustrations, street signs, mathematical symbols, and the editing language of film, for example. As they are absorbed over time, your struggle to grasp their meaning drops away, and you can "read" them with no conscious effort. As this happens, your understanding feels natural, and you begin to take the meaning of such things as obvious. The process is so well ingrained that we often don't realize after the fact that we have accepted a certain set of meanings for a given visual input. We don't always specifically learn them in textbooks or classrooms, but simply take them in through exposure to media. These meanings function after a while as a kind of ideology for the eye, to the point that we can hardly imagine that a flag, or a color, or a filmic image, could mean anything other than what we think it "should."

As mentioned above, this naturalization of signs, conventions, and codes is a shortcut for us who have to get along in society by instant and easy grasp of such things. Likewise, when a code is violated, you can actually experience a sense of unease. When audio codes like the rules of harmony are violated, for example, you experience dissonance, and when certain visual codes are violated, you actually might develop a sense of vertigo or even physical nausea. (See also the box titled "What Is a Mythologist?" in Chapter 7 for an example of how marketing and branding of soaps in the last century helped reinforce codes in which colors represent purity and cleaning power.)

Naturalization occurs at the levels of culture and politics as well. As Roland Barthes points out, some symbols in the culture are repeated so often and in the same political context (i.e., a convention for their use comes into being and becomes widespread) that people start to unquestioningly accept the validity of the symbols without questioning what they are being used for. National flags, images of femininity and masculinity, car chases in the movies, and cute animal memes are all naturalized signs in the culture that we tend to accept wholescale and without any kind of critical examination of what they mean, or how they might be used.

But as we continue to step away from privileging reading/ writing as a central, formal way of transmitting information, we must ask: what about visuality in general? Why *don't* our schools formally train us for years and years, as they do with reading and writing, how to recognize the conventions of visual production and interpretation? Art majors and art school students will often tell you they are desperately interested in making up for the years of elementary and secondary school training that devalue visual learning. Another way to think about it is that we may be actively schooled to learn and contemplate the elements of writing an essay, or grammar and spelling and vocabulary, or how to write a research paper, but we are generally not schooled in the elements of visual design, the conventions and codes of cinema, or how to tell a story in visual formats. Hence, visual modes are learned more through daily experience; we have relatively little specially developed conceptual vocabulary to question, study, or examine them, and thus they are harder to explain.

We'll return now to the idea of modes. A *mode* is a manner of experiencing, a way in which we absorb information, perhaps even what we might call a channel of communication. Hence, we have visual modes (text, color, watching a scene unfold in front of us), but also auditory or linguistic (spoken language), even olfactory (communication via scent and, to some extent, taste) or musical—which is in itself a kind of specialized mode somewhat akin to language. It is almost always possible (and indeed, often automatic) to interpret signs through multiple channels of meaning at once, which is an important part of what we mean when we talk about their multimodality. Modes can also be defined in more specific terms: we might subdivide the mode of *writing* into handwriting or print, subdividing each of these further (graffiti versus cursive, a text message versus a book). *Oral language* could be a conversation, or a rap performance. But if we think of *sound* as an overarching mode, we can also recognize that street noise, the buzz of machines, the sounds of animals, and even our own breathing are all signals that we use to interpret what is going on around us through *semiosis*, as discussed in Chapter 1. Likewise, the information we gain from touch can go beyond whether something is soft or hard, or cold or hot. For example, to make sense of wind blowing on our faces, we must interpret *haptic* modes that have to do with the literal sensations of the body, and *spatial* modes that relate to our awareness of our immediate environment. Spatial modes can be profoundly architecturally and cognitively complex and are another kind of way that humans organize information, then interpret it.

Any number of these modes can be crucial to meaning making and can give us multiple clues to what we think is going on as we interpret a "text." While our focus in this book is on the visual, it almost never occurs in isolation; when you regard a piece of text or an object in the world, you are also taking in sounds, smells, sensations, etc. A visuality-based concept of meaningful silence might be when you approach someone examining something carefully or gazing on beautiful scenery. Their silence informs our response to the situation: if they are concentrating or experiencing a private moment of awe, we might wait for them to talk first, or whisper or silently tiptoe away out of respect. (In terms of *naturalization*, this is the kind of behavior often codified in spaces like museums.) All of our knowledge of sound as a super-important mode tends to go into how we experience visual modes—even silent movies featured music as an aid to divining the movie makers' intentions, for example.

It is an interesting exercise to think of the various ways that visuality and its surrounding modes can be broken up into units or special ways of recognizing and interpreting information. For example, interpreting what you see while driving on the highway differs in very significant ways from interpreting what you see in a driving simulator or driving video game, even though they are all ostensibly "about" the same thing. (Note: we beg you to not get so distracted by interpreting elements of the road that you drive off it.) Likewise, some visual systems like those used in geometry or astronomy are highly specialized, with many special conventions that go beyond merely recognizing shapes and constellations. Geometry is itself a multimodal form: numbers and symbols form one mode of meaning-making, while diagrams and other spatial representations are another. The two sets of signs combine into the convention of recognizing geometry as an area of mathematics. Moreover, geometry's various modes must be specifically and carefully taught, learned, and practiced in order to be understood. This example also demonstrates that some kinds of meaning-making are more complex and challenging than others to talk about and grasp.

Each of the visual modes we encounter can be quite different, some of them requiring different kinds of education, cognitive abilities, and sensorial skills than others. Radiologists must go through long years of training and practice to learn how to read medical images accurately. Sharpshooters tend to have both extremely keen eyesight and an ability to imagine the trajectory of what they are shooting, drawing on—beyond that mysterious thing called *talent*—a well-trained sensitivity to visual, physical (in the sense of physics), and kinesic (in the sense of bodily movement) modes. Your ability to separate out and interpret visual information is also subject to your background and the kinds of experiences you have had. Those with less familiarity and training in how modes interact often have a hard time discerning the difference among the visual modes that they encounter, and can more easily be manipulated by word, image and sound. (Designers, illustrators, and the creators of propaganda and advertising are well aware of this.) Above all, modes are cultural; they are part of how we learn to be competent creators and interpreters of meaning. When we learn how to encode and decode information, we are learning how to use modes like the visual, the haptic, the aural, etc. to engage in meaning-making.

We want to point out that when determining how to label a mode, overarching terms (visual, written, aural, olfactory, spatial) can be useful, but as you zoom in on a meaning-making situation, it is perfectly fine to use your own intuition to come up with your own targeted labels for smaller units, phenomena, or items. In fact, whatever you are examining, you don't even really have to call their ways of transmitting information *modes* as long as you keep in mind that other scholars may be using the term to describe something very close to what you are looking at. Going beyond modes, each act of semiosis may be subject to conventions and codes, but also involves a specific history of prior meaning-making, as well as layers upon layers of producers, receivers, makers and interpreters, subjects and ideas, channels of uptake, and even important moments of misunderstanding. All of this has taken place before you even address the actual objects in front of you.

This chapter provides a rather broad definition of mode, and you may find that scholars with a specific purpose, like doing a critical film analysis or being present at a street protest, use the word in a narrower sense more tailored to their field. (The same actually happens with the terms *code* and *convention*, as mentioned above). Semioticians—that is, people doing media interpretation, as well as linguists examining language in everyday use—don't always worry too much about universal categories, but they do take care to provide their *operating* or *functional* definitions going into what they wish to analyze. You should start to think this way too. Always discuss up-front what kinds of parameters you are using to describe the thing you are trying to understand.

How Do Modes Interact?

There are a quite a few modes that appear frequently together and have their own conventions in combination, such as the visual and the verbal in journalism and in advertising. For example, Allan Bell demonstrates how both journalists and non-profits will use what are called "involvement photographs" as illustrations that are central to creating a sense of emotional engagement with the reader. Such photos involve the subject(s) of the photo looking directly at the camera, and thus, directly into the eyes of the reader. They create in the reader a sense of personal connection to the subject, and strongly increase buy-in or emotional interest in the subject of the written article. The use of involvement photos is highly conventionalized in journalism and advertising. (Note: the way we use involvement photo here is not quite the same as the photojournalists' involvement with the subject, although it can be related).

Take a look at the two photos in Image 5.2 of Syrian refugees taken in 2014. What kinds of written text do you expect they would be used with—journalistic, non-profit, educational, etc.?

IMAGE 5.2 Top: Involvement photo featuring Syrian refugee children; **bottom:** non-involvement group photo of a Syrian refugee group

What sort of multimodal meaning would be created as a result? The top photo featuring three boys looking directly at the camera are typical of involvement photos; we as viewers become "involved" on some level with the imagined intentions of the subjects. News features that wish to enhance the emotional uptake of their reportage will combine verbal modes like first-person stories with photographic modes like involvement images to more effectively have an interpersonal impact on their readers. Now look at the bottom photo, in which we as viewers do not make any kind of eye contact with the imagined subjects. Moreover, we are looking at them from a different plane. This non-involvement style of photo tends to have a lesser emotional impact on the viewer. Non-involvement photos are often chosen for "objective" news reporting—a different, but also powerful, journalistic approach.

EYE CONTACT FOR INDIVIDUALS AND POLITICIANS

Eye contact between people varies greatly, not only cross-culturally but across different groups within any one culture. Making eye contact has different social and persuasive implications and, as a highly visual practice, it accompanies oral language to help us recognize and interpret the potential meanings of what people are saying. Consider how we use codes of eye contact to regulate conversation in American or British contexts—is our conversation partner holding their eyes steady on one object or looking at our faces as we speak? Or is that partner looking around the room, or staring intently at the floor? The latter would say to us "I am not connecting to this person with my message."

But what about our more overt codes or expectations for eye contact? Staring someone straight in the eyes can be either perceived as a threat—"who are YOU looking at?" is a warning to back off—or as a statement of connection and importance as when people "see something eye to eye." Consider for example, how truthfulness is or is not connected to making direct eye contact in your own culture group. Likewise, staring someone down can be seen as an act of declaring superiority, or conversely, looking superiors straight in the eye can feel like a challenge to the social order. Such staring can make people in subordinate positions or people who are subject to bullying acutely uncomfortable or even fearful. People who have difficulty with eye contact are often taught overtly how to recognize and use the eye contact norms of people in their culture, or other cultures, in order to better interpret and respond to what is going on around them.

Politicians may in fact be coached carefully in how to manage eye contact, in order to appear non-threatening in their visual contact (smile!) and to connect to the people they are immediately communicating with. Importantly, when images of politicians in interaction are interpreted by the public, photos that show eye contact situations can convince voters of the politicians' sense of caring and intelligence. A skilled politician who makes direct eye contact by looking into a camera, speaking out to their audiences on the other side of the screen, will effectively convey immediacy and direct connection to their constituents.

When we consider *aural* or hearing modes, music and lyrics are two that occur so frequently together that their conventions are easily absorbed by the very young; most of us learn to sing as toddlers in the home, and much of children's interaction with both people and media involves singing. Music videos add additional sub-modes like the art of dance and may be connected to advertising or memes (and frequently feature a *male gaze*, as mentioned in Chapter 4). The presentation and performance of all these modes around music and lyrics are highly conventionalized, with clear codes/rules for the kinds of performances people expect to see. If they did not, then the judges (including you) on *American Idol* or *Eurovision* would have a hard time collectively choosing who was best.

Spatial modes are also highly significant for visuality, because beyond a multimodal object itself, our ideas of looking within different spaces can alter the process of seeing and reading texts. The refugee photos above create slightly different effects in the viewer if they are seen in the context of this book, or as printouts on glossy photo paper in a gallery or in a religious space. Similarly, viewing them at home is different from viewing them in the classroom; which space will demand more attention or a certain emotional response? The discourses around the kind of behavior (i.e., the *conventions*) suited to each space include norms around the way we perceive what is within them. Depending on who we are as individuals, our reaction to those norms will cause the spatial mode to have a very personalized impact on the reading.

Some modes do not frequently interact, or only interact in particular instances. The olfactory and the visual may interact when eating a special meal, but with the exception of Scratch'n'Sniff books or magazine perfume samples, the visual mode of reading written language is not generally paired with aromas. However, there are some multimodal experiences we talk about that are more subjective. Take *pleasure reading*, for example. For one person, it might only involve a combination of visual submodes (reading a novel on your tablet) with haptic ones (sitting in a comfortable chair). For another, it might involve the olfactory, say, if they need a scented candle in the room to consider it pleasure reading. Some of these ways of experiencing the world have hard boundaries for how we define them, while others are more flexible.

This attention to submodes has become even more useful today than in the past, given the ways that new technologies have allowed us to share highly visual texts, combining modes in novel, but increasingly common and newly conventionalized ways. YouTube tutorial videos, a thread of shared images like pet pages, emoticon jokes on social media, and widespread but specifically branded technologies for video-calling are all examples of things that combine visual and other modes in specific ways, and that have developed codes and conventions through their communities of use that deserve our attention. We will discuss some of these novel challenges for multimodal interpretation in the next chapter (6), particularly around memes. Chapter 7 also explains ways that specially combined visual modes on social media can connect us psychologically to political movements.

Reading a Multimodal Text or Object

We want to reinforce some of the ideas in the preceding sections by giving you a thorough look at a single, complex, multimodal text—which, if you'll remember, can be much more than just a set of words. Consider the "text" in Image 5.3.

This photo was taken by one of the authors in summer 2020, when protests sparked by the murder of George Floyd swept across the United States and other nations, along with a surge in support for the Black Lives Matter movement. Many murals and artistic texts like this one, located in Philadelphia, appeared in cities around the world. At a broad level, a passerby would recognize that this *sign*—for indeed, it conveys a lot of visual information with text and image—is a piece of artwork. We might say that the primary *convention* for a piece of artwork is to display it so others can see, and that the cultural *code* is to stand and examine it. Depending on the content of the piece, the onlooker might feel admiration, or indifference, or sorrow, or some other emotion. Different cultures also have different standards around realism in art (in keeping with our earlier

IMAGE 5.3 Store front mural in South Philadelphia

discussion of photography in Chapter 4), and strong opinions about street art of various kinds. Nevertheless, anyone outside of this storefront would recognize this moment as being more like standing in a gallery than simply pausing on the sidewalk.

In the work itself, the artist has used text and image to create a powerful statement. The boy (whose youth is indicated by his stuffed lion) has an almost inscrutable expression as he looks upward; his shirt is inscribed with BLACK LIVES MATTER, which when combined with the color of his skin, is too often enough a signal for some people to pass judgment. Behind him, each brick is inscribed with the name of a Black individual killed by the police, echoing the "Say his/her/their name(s)" chants common at street protests. It is noteworthy that high-profile names from cases in the last several years (Trayvon Martin, Eric Garner, Philando Castile ...) are thoroughly mixed with names that have received less attention. The names of George Floyd and Breonna Taylor, perhaps the two most familiar ones from the first half of 2020, are located in areas that we tend to look toward while reading: the top left and the center. Yet neither is given a spotlight over the other names, and in a way, the effect of a wall of names blurring together is more powerful than trying to go through each one. The names spilling off the edge of the "canvas," and the repeated uniformity of brickwork, suggest the endless monotony of the social wrong that the artist is addressing. (One other that does stand out is Tamir Rice, who was shot and killed by a police officer at age 12, and whose name is directly next to the child's face. Perhaps this highlights the exceptional tragedy of this incident among a series of exceptionally tragic incidents.)

Other aspects are more symbolic. The dove flying overhead is a well-known symbol for peace, but its sorrowful expression, tears, and the scrap of police tape in its beak make its role ambiguous here. Is it breaking down the wall to show the colorful sky behind? Or is the wall still in progress, with bricks like the ones next to the child waiting to be added? The meaning of the piles of apples are less clear to us, but the blood is unmistakable; perhaps it is a callback to the well-known anti-lynching song, "Strange Fruit." But you can see how even for us, the authors, our interpretations aren't completely certain. We get the gist of it, and we are emotionally impacted by the piece, but we read this text through the lens of being white academics living in "blue" areas of the country. The cultural codes we were naturalized into, and the ways they align with politics, lead us to conclusions that are no doubt different from those that others might arrive at—some slightly different, some wildly.

The *hypermediacy* of the work also lends itself to multimodal examination. Obviously, this is not a real brick wall, and the visibility of the door handles indicates what this surface is normally used for. (Hypermediacy is defined further in Chapter 6, but for our purposes here, it means a message that calls attention to itself as media or made up of mediums.) The image is painted on paper, but applied to the door with wheat paste, a mixture of flour and water whose use for street art has grown rapidly in popularity in Philadelphia. At the bottom left of the image, the words "#tagyourblock" appear, giving us another example of sign, convention, and code. The # symbol, or hashtag, has become universally recognized as a marker of digital life, especially for platforms like Twitter and Instagram. When hashtagged words appear in the corner of a work of street art like this, much like an artist's signature, the convention is that this piece is somehow the property of, or at least strongly associated with, those words. (The absence of a signature here is telling; the artist is anonymous but is projecting this piece into a specific corner of the digital landscape, represented by this tag.) The code, in turn, is to go searching for pieces with this tag online, and to perhaps create one's own, as part of a highly salient new submode of internet culture.

Finally, there is a degree of preexisting knowledge that exists outside the frame of the piece, which can add further context. Note that the wheat pasted painting has been applied to plywood, which is affixed to the doors and windows, along with a metal grille on the left side. During the protests, Philadelphia experienced property damage and looting, leading many business owners in heavily-trafficked areas of the city to board up their windows. This storefront is located just off South Street, a very popular shopping and nightlife area, but one that had not seen any major demonstrations at the time this photo was taken. Several other establishments nearby had similarly boarded up their windows, though few used them as canvases like this. We might read a political stance in the choice of medium here: the owner of this building is worried about vandalism (which in the United States, and especially in the context of Black Lives Matter, is highly racialized in the public discourse), and believes that protesters might target their store. But in an effort not to seem like they are valuing property above the moral imperative that the protesters stand for, they have commissioned this mural to show support. It's a delicate political line to walk and muddies the waters further about how we should interpret this artwork.

We could go further—there are other painted elements to the left and right of this central panel to explore, and more that could be said about the dynamics between the producer and consumer of the text—but this analysis probably suffices to make our point that even a single encounter on the street like this can be rich with significance. Importantly, so much of the symbolic, emotional, and political connections we make when we see a mural like this happen quickly, and often semiconsciously. A passerby needs only a few seconds' glance to get the major ideas here, and maybe half a minute to stand there and deeply consider the work to draw all the conclusions, or something similar, that we have just listed. In that sense, it may seem like we are digging more deeply than we need to; our rejoinder is that so many disciplines, most notably art history, have produced entire volumes of analysis about works much less complex on the surface than this. Our point is not that you *should* stop and consider signs you encounter this deeply, but that you already *do*, often without realizing it. Our visuality and our brains are remarkable things.

Parting Comment on Multimodal Interpretation

Social scientists, linguists, and psychologists are drawn to multimodal readings of complex meaning-making efforts because they combine microscopic or *micro-interactive* analyses of small items within the visual field with *macro-interactive* or big picture questions. There are certainly other ways and methods to study the meaning and function of something like murals. For example, if you were a tour guide, you could record their size, distribution, and subject matter for visitors to your city, or interview tourists about what they glean from these objects and how they interpret them. You might search Instagram to see which ones have been the most popular spots for people to take photos of their own, *remediating* the painted surface of a storefront into a digital selfie. But working inductively from a specific context or example is a powerful way to learn about how people use modes, from combinations of objects, texts, and visual stimuli, to buildings and rooms and other spaces, to make meaning. Applying these observational techniques to what you encounter in everyday life can also help you understand better the combinatory technologies around such items. It is an ideal method for grasping new forms of meaning-making as they appear and are used in real-time. Ultimately, multimodal analysis is particularly strong at grasping how visual images combine with other *kinds of meanings* and other *ways of making meaning* to create new forms of communication.

Exercises

1. Think of a daily or weekly task that you do in a specific place. From your own memory, write down what you think are the conventions of interpreting/understanding the multiple modes of information that one must use to perform that task. Then go, do that task in person yourself; take a photo during the process, and keep notes on how others seem interpret that place, space, or experience. (Depending on the task you choose, you might be able to get this information as you do it, or just by showing the photo to friends afterwards and asking what they think.) What did you get right? What did you get wrong? Trade with a partner. How different was your partner's write up from yours, and what did they appreciate that you didn't, and vice versa? Give your partner feedback.

2. We can now record history as moving images, instead of written versions or paintings. Find a combat image or video from the last 50 years and compare that to the portrayal of battles of the Burgundian Wars in Image 3.5. How do the contemporary and much older versions compare? How does the enhanced multimodality of the contemporary battle you found compare to the color and size modes of the Burgundian Wars (note that both of the images are roughly the size of 8x10 paper)? Finally, consider how reading about battles is different than visually absorbing these images?

3. Look around carefully the next time you visit a public commercial space like a mall or downtown shopping district, or even a commercial website. Consider how products are arranged on shelves, in windows, etc. How does the way the space is set up affect your view of them? Think about angles and lines of sight relative to your height, how close you can get to the products, whether there is any intervening object like a pane of glass, a computer screen, etc. How do you think you would view objects, advertisements, and other elements in a commercial landscape differently if they were in a different context? You might try visiting a physical store, and then visiting their website, to see how the same items are displayed differently.

For Further Exploration

Bell, Allan. (1998). *Approaches to News Discourse.* Hoboken, NJ: Wiley-Blackwell.

• Selected chapters explore multimodal meaning between written text, visual image, and television broadcast.

Kress, Gunther, & Theo van Leeuwen. (2001). Multimodal discourse. *The Modes and Media of Contemporary Communication.* New York, NY: Bloomsbury.

• Short and accessible "classic" in how multimodality works.

Pennycook, Alistair, & Emi Otsuji. (2015). *Metrolingualism: Language in the City*. New York, NY: Routledge.

• An exploration of how many different modes affect our individual interactions with signage and language in cityscapes.

Thomson, T.J. (2019). *To See and Be Seen: The Environments, Interactions and Identities behind News Images*. London, UK: Rowman and Littlefield.

• Discusses the factors that go into the creation and dissemination of news images, as well as the impact on both subjects and audiences.

6

REMEDIATION AND INTERTEXUALITY

Introduction

As this book has so far highlighted how the production, reception, and interpretation of images is subject to many conditions, some of which are more overtly conscious and directed than others. We have discussed the role that the following play in visual meaning-making and interpretation: biology and cognition; cultural and religious-philosophical ideologies; established conventions and codes of meaning-making; technological factors (more information on technology is coming in this and the next few chapters); the multimodal aspects of how images and other kinds of meaning-making activities are combined; and finally, the ways that images are subjected to codes and conventions in context. This chapter focuses on what happens when images are placed in new contexts and how *remediation* itself is a special form of human communication. Briefly, *remediation* refers to ideas about how an image (or other kinds of meaningful content) is picked up and moved into a new context, acquiring new meanings in the process, sometimes as a direct result of being shifted into an entirely new medium. This replication may also direct the image towards different audiences and different purposes. As you may imagine, recent major technological changes like social media and the ubiquity of cell phone cameras have enhanced the role that remediation of the visual plays in human culture.

The *media* in remediation refers to the **channels** and **forms** that the image or other content passes through as it is reproduced and repurposed. For visual information, *channels* of media could mean cameras, social media formats, televisions, laptops and tablets, print, etc.—anything a meaningful image or text must pass through before it reaches us. As for media *forms*, these refer to the actual object that we see, which could be one of a vast number of things: ink on paper, paint, printed photos, or such as gifs, memes, pixels, posters, flyers, 3D movies, and so forth. In the process of changing an item with meaningful form so that it can be delivered along a new channel, or a new format, new meanings are generated. They can influence human perception and communication in novel ways.

Following the developmental arc of photography, moving pictures, videotape, instantly developing photo prints, and mobile phone cameras, our featured example for discussing remediation and intertextuality in this chapter are memes. They are another next step in a series of innovations that have increased the ease of reproducing and circulating images in new channels and forms, this time through social media and the internet. Although visual remediation itself did not start with the advent of online culture, it takes on new kinds of weight and meaning through digital programs and devices. Remediation of images in various online sharing platforms is now a phenomenon of immense social, cultural, and political influence.

On Intertextuality

The practice of remediating images, re-creating them in new media environments, is also an example of *intertextuality*. Intertextuality is the idea that all texts—broadly defined to include image, sounds, and words, almost anything that signifies or carries specific meaning—are interconnected. You can see this at a basic level when one text quotes or refers to another, or more subtly when we expand upon the definition of *genre* from Chapter 4. The conventions of a genre such as a horror film (which is a text in the sense we mean here) are only recognizable if the viewer understands how they link to and borrow from other horror films. But when a text is reproduced and altered, it is still connected to its previous form; portions of its earlier meaning are brought along with it. Thus, our interpretations can be carried from one text to another, across words, images and sounds that are slightly altered versions of themselves. In a sense, intertextuality is a fairly obvious idea; if we produced something completely new, with no elements of the past in it, we would have no conventions to rely on to interpret it. There are a few rare moments in history where something almost completely novel has appeared, but ultimately, almost everything is meaningful because it has long been situated within the discourse of human experience and action. Intertextuality is also not just about media, but could be about a hand gesture, a dance step, the design of a desk, patterns on fabric, architectural form, and so forth. Intertextuality is the acknowledgement that each text has a life of meaning-making embedded in time and space as it is repeated, changed, and connected to other texts.

Intertextuality is also a persuasive force, where previous *powers* of words, images, and ideas can carry over into the latest expression through a long chain of textual re-presentation. A mundane example would be that of someone expressing a greeting through a smile or a head nod in a way appropriate to their culture. Each time that gesture is used, its persuasive force of expressing the mutual recognition of another person is part of a long chain of reproducing, recognizing, and interpreting that gesture, one that straightforwardly binds together society. Consider also, for example, your reaction to well-known images of horror, as opposed to horrific images that you encounter for the first time. Images of war, accidents, or victims of violent death that we have seen before have the additional weight of both their cultural recognition and their long chain of accruing and reproducing meanings of pain, suffering, and fear.

Images that are very culturally iconic, like Leonardo DaVinci's fresco of the *Last Supper*, accrue powerful meaning over all the years of their reproduction and uptake by Western (and now non-Western) audiences. If you look over the meme in Image 6.1, you'll see that the very power of the image is made

"Last Supper," by Leonardo da Vinci, revised for Zoom.

IMAGE 6.1 Last Supper Meme; here the "text" of the Last Supper and what it signifies about care, sacrifice, and death is juxtaposed to the "text" of a possibly deadly boring Zoom meeting

humorous when it is juxtaposed to a more recent text, that of the "gallery view" screen in the video meeting platform, Zoom. For those of you unfamiliar with the latter, during the COVID-19 pandemic of 2020, Zoom rose to prominence because it allowed big institutions, such as workplaces, city governments, corporations, etc., to easily connect with large numbers of employees and other people; the company made it easy for individuals to use privately as well. During Zoom meetings, windows with participants on camera would substitute for the presence of people during a live meeting format. The Last Supper Meme gets its humor from combining the importance of a deep and meaningful moment in Christian history and belief with the mundane, even boring, experience of spending hours listening to people in the relatively non-dynamic computer environment that is an online meeting. The power of the mundane meets the power of God, so to speak, in this intertextual joke.

From Memes to Internet Memes

In their original conception by the biologist Richard Dawkins, long before the internet was a popular phenomenon, a *meme* was simply an idea or point of cultural reference that could be spread from person to person. He discussed them in biological term: memes could evolve, mutate, or go extinct. Social media policy analyst Jonathan L. Zittrain defines memes today as "a picture or drawing (usually from an unwitting source) that's taken on a shared, iconic quality, coupled with a resonating message" (p. 388). Note that when Zittrain uses the word *iconic* here, he does not mean it in the sense of resemblance to the real as a semiotician would use it, but rather he is using it in its popular sense of "cultural icon," something that has wide social recognition, and cultural cachet. The definition also captures the special persuasive powers of memes when he goes on to say that a "meme at its best exposes a truth about something and in its versatility allows that truth to be captured and applied in new situations" (p. 389). Besides popular and resonating messages that seem to capture and apply truths in new situations, memes are often in the hands of regular people, and widely shared person to person. This is what we mean when we say that memes are examples of *participatory culture*.

But Dawkins and Zittrain's definitions don't take into account how memes are involved with technology. For example, memes of the 1970s were enabled by the abundance of office supplies such as scotch tape and correction fluid, while the mimeograph and the copy machine facilitated memes being duplicated for sharing. Prior to these technologies, replicating an image and shifting its meanings through subtle intertextual means was technologically out of reach for the average person. Consider the contrast between the participatory aspects of memes in the 1970s and graffiti. Graffiti is as old as humanity's various modes of writing—some of the tombs of ancient Egypt are downright covered in it—and re-working figures and images with transgressive art is of course also a widespread intertextual practice in the history of meaning-making. But memes derive much of their power from the technology that is used to create and infinitely reproduce them. Their technological replicability is a major part of both their effectiveness and their appeal.

The give-and-take relationship between memes and technology is especially visible with the rise of *internet memes*, which have flourished as new systems of visual creation, platforms for sharing, and new online communities have appeared. The construction and circulation of memes has become ever easier, and their creators can reach large and diverse audiences across much greater distances than circulating a mimeograph or a photocopy in the office, neighborhood, or local bar. Likewise, internet programs affect users, and users make choices about using technology that end up shaping messages in turn. Not only are meme generators and social media platforms new forms of technological replicability in and of themselves, but they are also part of a set of technological parameters that determine how we might interact with images, along with size, image quality, amount of additive text, shareability, audience reception, and so forth.

The change and growth of memes is largely subject to a given platform's *affordances*, the specific features of digital interfaces that determine what we can or cannot do with them. These include the mechanical options (can you "like" a meme, or easily click a button to "share" it?), but also social behaviors that lead users to certain patterns of sharing behavior (one might want to share some memes in a broadly accessible social media space, and other memes with selected groups of friends via a messaging option). A social network's offerings eventually align with its participants' abilities and inclinations to use social media; the interface and the user start to affect each other's ways of creating social contact on the web. So for example, most social media have the option to evaluate a posted item positively and/or negatively. People may choose to share a meme in one program or platform over another, based on these evaluative elements, or perhaps on other affordances (like how images disappear quickly in social media like Snapchat). The differences between platforms affect how memes are spread, seen, and interpreted worldwide; how do memes travel on Instagram versus Twitter versus Facebook versus WhatsApp? Yet users always manage to find a way to work within each set of affordances. As a result, all of these issues are central to examining how remediation occurs and how it affects meaning.

Illustration: The Firestarter Meme

Consider the "Firestarter" internet meme (Image 6.2), one of the most widely circulated in the early 2000s, around the time that internet memes began to take off through email sharing, web repositories, and then social media. It is a particularly strong example of the interesting properties of memes created in the era of the internet, arising at a moment when meme generators, image upload capacity, and user attention were all coming together to function as new affordances within online networks.

IMAGE 6.2 Examples of the "Firestarter/Disaster Girl" meme

Memes initially ask us to do some basic visual and historical interpretation, just like we might do with a framed photograph on display. The Firestarter meme requires background cultural knowledge of (originally European) holiday practices, in which poorly behaved children are given lumps of coal as an annual holiday gift instead of the desirable items their well-behaved peers receive. Like many memes, some irony is used to make this humorous. We see that an ill-mannered child—one look at her face tells us she is up to something—has taken her punishment for bad behavior and amplified it into even worse behavior by burning down a house. This meme, in particular, expresses the essential idea of powerless people turning the tables to exercise some kind of alternative power (even if it might be negative or naughty power).

The photo of a child down the street from a burning house that stands as the basis for this meme was created improvisationally, even though the image appears to be purposefully and carefully crafted. Its resemblance to a film outtake is reflected by the meme's two most common labels: "Disaster Girl" and "Firestarter," the latter of which is a reference to a 1984 motion picture about a child with supernatural powers. Thus, it has a vaguely intertextual feel of deriving power from a movie. In fact, we hesitated to use this meme because it seemed like the source photo may have been either a proprietary image belonging to a movie studio, or perhaps a private image that invades the privacy of this 4-year-old girl to invite less-than-charitable comments about her supposed poor behavior. However, learning the backstory of the meme helped clear up these ethical concerns.

The photo was taken by photographer Dave Roth. Roth and his daughter Zoe, the girl pictured in the meme, both know of its popularity on the web and have remarked publicly that they do not mind its being shared. The Roths had heard a commotion on their street and came out to see a fire in one of the neighbor's houses. Dave had his camera and took photos of his children and the fire, eventually publishing the photo of Zoe in *JPG Magazine* online. *JPG Magazine* posted the photo on their homepage, from which it was picked up by unknown individuals and made into a meme. In a 2016 interview, the Roths told a web news reporter that the image has made them famous but not gained them any money, an indication of how unpredictable the monetization of online content can be. Zoe's image eventually was given the nickname "Disaster Girl"; the real Zoe and her friends have long made light-hearted fun of the popularity of the meme as a cultural phenomenon (Green, 2016).

Internet memes travel easily across social networks. They are arguably an intrinsic part of social networks on the web. With about half of the world's population engaged in some form of social media as of 2020, they also travel globally, crossing language and cultural barriers among members of many social groups. For example, the lower right panel of Image 6.2 shows the Disaster Girl Meme in Spanish. The translation goes *I told him: "I wanted my meme to be popular again" and he said: "Over my dead body."*

The most widely used memes also may have a long life and importantly, they become self-referential or meta-memes. Take a look at the *Titanic* version of the Disaster Girl meme (upper right corner of Image 6.2). One has to have familiarity with the original Firestarter meme as well as an idea about the visual and historical significance of the *Titanic* in order to pick up on what the picture of the young child signifies. The self-reference of the meme becomes noticeable in other ways. For example, look at how in the "Remember disaster girl?" image (lower left corner of Image 6.2), an adult Zoe Roth is contrasted to her earlier self. For those who do remember the original meme, we have an almost personal, birthday-card-like connection with the girl in the image. Disaster Girl or perhaps Zoe herself has become a new sort of cultural icon.

All of this illustrates different things about how memes "work" to amuse, inform, or otherwise affect us. To put it another way, the immediate work of interpreting a meme involves an encounter with the version in front of the viewer's face, but that experience is also knowingly contrasted with the viewer's knowledge of the image being remediated. Literally, we use the fact that a meme is a meme to enhance the experience of interpreting it. This is related to the concept of intertexuality in that the accrued meaning of one of these items comes in part from its long chain of repetition. There is a twofold remediation in this case: generating an internet meme by reproducing a photograph on the internet, with filters and novel written texts, and sharing it through social media channels, whose different affordances add different shades of meaning to any one iteration of the image. Moreover, there is a special kind of persuasive status that stems from the label of "meme"; we sometime seek out memes as a preferred way to share various messages about our beliefs and ideas of identification.

But there is yet another quality to social media and image that is a profound part of basic human communication. Memes and other images that are widely shared among people (whether they know each other or not) have in common what is called the *phatic function* in communication, where a shared point of communication—a laugh, a smile, a nod of understanding—unites disparate minds within the human condition, regardless of the message's actual content. What is of central importance in phatic communication is to create a sense of social connection, rather than the transfer of referential information. There is a "we all have been there" feeling to this meme, perhaps as witnesses to naughty behavior, perhaps as spectators to a fire, or perhaps as audience members experiencing the *Firestarter* movie. Social media are sometimes just like other phatic forms—small talk, laughing at a physical comedy routine, joking, and certain forms of politeness—tapping into this human need for phatic sharing. It is part of the collective nature of "truth" in the definition of memes mentioned above.

Hypermediacy and the Metavisual

Between phatic functions of image sharing, and the notion that images have an immediate or being-present-in-the-moment quality, it is clear that images themselves mediate human connection. We feel directly connected to images as they are encountered and interpreted, and that direct connection extends to involve others who experience it as well—oddly, even if we don't know them personally. This is one of the reasons why "likes" and other signs of approbation in social media are so important, as well as when someone we don't know makes a joke or a slogan to which we can relate, we feel a form of connection.

However, that's only half the story when it comes to the social sharing of images and how people use them. There is often a gap between the feeling of connection and the sense of reality in an image, and our recognition of the image as a product of conscious action or as a product of technology. This awareness is called *hypermediacy*: the tendency of a medium to highlight its own nature *as* a medium. This is easily seen in a painting where each brushstroke is clearly visible, or that is made up of words that says "this is a painting," or in a movie that uses the effect of the film coming loose from the projector or burning through, or in a television show that starts with a family watching a television show, etc. Much of the pleasure and social force of remediation involves contrasting immediacy with hypermediacy, where new media simultaneously call attention to their difference from the old, and also present themselves as providing a newer, better, (usually) visual experience. Memes illustrate this phenomenon by overtly evoking their original form, but also playing meaningfully on themselves in their production and delivery to friends and acquaintances, foes and enemies, alike. The fact that we both forget the presence of the medium when we are experiencing it, yet also see and experience things about it that remind us of its nature as a reproduction or remediation, is essential to understanding how media affect us.

There's another special but related tension with the immediate and the hypermediate, arising from technology that can make images and visual representation both abstract and highly iconic (in the semiotic sense as described in Chapter 1) or realistic. We often seem to prefer, especially in the West, images that produce a realistic feeling of "being there," and will choose concrete images over abstract images much of the time. With each new visual technology, we can do fantastic things with images, and yet we tend to try to manipulate them for "realism" rather than let too much of their seeming falsity come through. When that falsity becomes too obvious, the tension between the immediate and hypermediate loses its force. Thus, science fiction movies, fight scenes, and electronic portraiture all tend to retain key aesthetic features in presenting people, outer space, and so forth that have a "reality" quality to them, even if they are in a sense entirely "false." Similar to how we discussed vision as separate from but crucial to visuality, our brain is programmed to comfortably accept a certain level of realism, no more, no less. One well-known phenomenon is the "uncanny valley," where seeing human-like figures that are just slightly "off" generates revulsion in many viewers. (A compelling theory is that this stems from an instinctual aversion to corpses, whence zombie horror.) This psychological effect is relevant in a wide variety of fields, from robot design to creating characters for sci-fi films; the aesthetics of media must account for the emotional responses that images will create.

Because memes are self-referential, recreating and re-situating the original text through each derivative version, they do not trigger this feeling of separation from reality. In fact, seeing a new spin on a meme can make a viewer feel as though they're in on the joke; a new version of it is still the same meme. Meme remediation is not about directly improving a visual experience and obscuring the change, but rather remixing it and highlighting the difference. To an extent, to fully "get" a meme requires having seen at least a couple iterations of it before and appreciating the cleverness of its latest form of self-referentiality. Think about the first time you saw a popular meme versus the second, versus the tenth; regardless of how often the creators hit the sweet spot of being funny, politically relevant, etc., each version deepens your connection to the text.

Memes are also notable for the **metavisual** qualities that their creators tap into. The prefix *meta*-literally means "above" or "beyond" in Greek, but in this instance, a better translation might be "about." Thus, metavisual texts are to some degree about their own visuality; meta-advertising is advertising that is about being an advertisement; metacognitive refers to thinking that about thinking; metalinguistics is language about language, and so forth. Memes are metavisual to begin with because their very structure calls attention to their replication; they declare and charm us with the hypermediate commentary about *other replications* of themselves. The metavisual is built overtly into memes, occurring when and where we see that a single constant element of meaning is transported across contexts to signify new things visually. Because of its popular recognition in the culture, the Firestarter girl's image alone can be pulled out and attached to another widely recognized visual content element— the image of the *Titanic* sinking—and suddenly we have the Disaster Girl. The combination of memes, one modern and one historical, is so funny precisely because it plays on the joke that we already know these images from two very different sources so well. They are images *about* images, which is the essence of metavisuality.

What Do We Use Memes for? A Global Approach

We have alluded to the persuasive nature of memes throughout this chapter. Each remix of a meme or other visual item such as a photo, painting, etc. can have specific persuasive strategies and goals depending on the argumentative force that the producer and affordances give it. Memes cross social lines, international lines, and maybe even lines of politeness. They can be used in any number of political and persuasive and interpersonal contexts, often with the same meme espousing opposite sides of an issue, but with the same level of moral or emotional emphasis or force.

International comparative work on memes by Asaf Nissenbaum and Limor Shifman in Chinese, English, Spanish, and German contexts show that the majority of memes involve emotional expression around anger, happiness, and sadness, with some variation between the groups who use those languages. For example, all of the meme users in these global samples often used anger against groups in the abstract, using mainstream or *hegemonic* (see Chapter 8 for extended discussion) stereotypes against women and minorities. Nissenbaum and Shifman note that in these instances, memes are often "socially conservative but emotionally disruptive" (p. 294). The conservative and mainstream nature of memes may be because the initial creators of any given meme tend to be middle-class (and outside of China, white) men with enough know-how, access to technology and spare time to create and launch various memes. Additionally, for expressions of happiness, English, Spanish, and German meme users tended to mitigate or undercut their own expressions of happiness when choosing memes, often expressing self-ridicule, stressing the pettiness or insignificance of their own feelings. Earnest sadness was most often expressed in Chinese language memes.

There are other fascinating aspects that highlight the globalized and localized contexts for affordances, culture and the behavior of meme users. The English-, Spanish- and German-speaking meme users *all* tended to draw their **meme templates** (i.e., the visual item from which the meme will be created; Disaster Girl/Firestarter is a technically a template) from similar references, usually internationally recognized (but Western in origin) popular icons and current popular culture images. They also have close similarities in their stances toward others, resulting in criticism of groups or general behaviors, rather than expressions of deeply personal conflict with others. However, the localized contexts do often come through—for example, when Mexican TV show features unfamiliar to non-Spanish speaking consumers appear in Spanish memes. But Chinese users largely tended to deploy simplified cartoon memes, into which celebrity faces were inserted. These meme forms create rather specific modes for cultural expression, which users tend to make into statements about interpersonal relations.

Although memes get part of their power from how they tap into the broad human experience, as described around the Firestarter meme, or play to human emotion, as seen in the work of Nissenbaum and Shifman, memes can also have a dark side. Sometimes their persuasive and emotive power is used to shore up micro-communities online that serve far right agendas or used as personalized attacks on individuals who have become symbolic in a political or social cause. One originally neutral meme is the cartoon frog Pepe, derived from a 2005 comic by Matt Furie. The Pepe character image became a widespread meme in the 2010s, probably because his face seems *so* neutral that it takes textual captions to make him out to be "sad" or "angry" or any other emotion. Rather quickly, semi-private and curated social media groups picked up on Pepe and began to share him as an Alt-Right symbol—that is, he became a rallying symbol for extreme right activists who fomented ideas of white nationalism, antisemitism, and antifeminism online. Pepe was so effectively taken up in these circles that his image was ultimately put on the list of hate symbols maintained by the United States Anti-Defamation League, a nonprofit group that documents hate speech. Yet Pepe also became a meme signifying liberty and freedom of speech in the Hong Kong protests of 2019, demonstrating the fluidity of memes' meanings across different contexts.

Ultimately, the tale of Pepe and other memes is that they function in a relatively small number of ways having to do with the paradoxes of anonymity, powerlessness, and the need for recognition. They are sometimes shared symbolically in order to criticize dominant or powerful institutions (the online Alt Right remains largely anonymous and underground, after all), or to express general derision against others, or to express the feelings of despair, joy, sadness and other emotions of people who might otherwise feel their experiences are isolated or unacknowledged. These little electronic clusters of pixel and programming often have a surprising impact on us, individually and socially.

Memes, Copyright, and Privacy

We have already alluded to the circulation of images without paying royalties to the people who made those images. Indeed, each image in this book had to be carefully cleared with either its creator or copyright holder, or both, before Routledge would allow it to go press. That clearance involved receiving permission to print an image or paying a fee for fair use to the image copyright holder. (See box titled *What Are the Rules when It Comes to Image Copyright?* for more information about how this works.)

Because of new technologies of duplication and remediation, the obviousness of copyright is not always apparent to users of internet and smartphone social sharing platforms. It is quite literally so easy to share, or cut and paste images (and text, and sounds) from digital formats, that people worldwide tend to share copyrighted images without knowing they are engaging in an illegal act. Easy replication and circulation are both at the center of meme culture and at the center of the contemporary problems of copyright. Moreover, the wide availability of free meme creator programs on the web also seems to say to us "go ahead and circulate that image you found somewhere." Considering how anyone can play with memes and circulate/remediate them, lack of respect for copyright feels like something possibly creative and powerful. That is, generating and using memes is a way to directly harness the democratic qualities of user-generated content on the web, or as a personal expressive creative art form, something that resists or sidesteps the mass production and private ownership of media products.

Source images for memes are sometimes drawn from images with no direct connections to specific people. Many source images are connected to certain celebrities or actors playing a character whose special status and recognition in a sense isolates the individual from potential damage or shame when a meme is mean-hearted or hyper-critical. But many memes are built around family photographs, candid shots, or paparazzi or closed-circuit television images that invade peoples' privacy. Some incorporate potentially embarrassing images that their subjects probably never thought would be circulated online, and the very worst images are often humiliating. Does the right to privacy include the right to have control over how one is depicted in a public forum?

If memes work, in part, because they tap into a universally recognizable subject matter, then technically meme creators should all be able to find images that serve their purposes without hurting individuals featured in images. Likewise, Zoe Roth did not seem to be troubled about being Firestarter girl (she gave us direct permission to use her image in this book) and her case shows how the rich productivity of meme images from the confluence of individual image production is an important form of social creativity and social meaning making in the early 21st century. But many memes are used to attack specific people or ideas, and often they are offensive or invasive of privacy, or both. In fact, educational institutions and workplaces are starting to evolve policies around image use and harassment and even hate speech. Interestingly, these policies tend to be based not on the creation of memes *per se*, but on intent of the maker and placement or use of images in wider contexts: did you show this to a co-worker in order to attack or humiliate someone? These cases get a lot of attention, and some do a lot of damage socially and individually, but they are relatively few in number when one considers how many memes are circulated daily across the planet. Most memes blow over quickly, to the relief of any of their subjects who do not want the attention. But it raises the question of whether sharing is an ethical decision, and whether the boundary between a person's private life and the public sphere should be in the hands of the collective internet.

Conclusion

Keep in mind that any social media and other communication technology like texting, making posters and signs, and embedding images in mass media are affected by the idea of visual affordances as mentioned above. Memes are special because they are easily replicable and can be manipulated and shareable in specific ways that their users appreciate as part of internet culture. We focus on memes but encourage readers to think about how selfies or GIFs, emoticons or emoji, mass media photographs or YouTube videos are all subject to the effects of hypermediacy, and intertextuality in interpretation.

The constantly shifting landscape of digital media means that there are always new platforms in which memes and other visual items can be generated and shared. As they transition from one to the next, they retain some of their essence, lose whatever meaning they had that was specific to the old space (such as how Pepe lost some of his alt-right veneer when appropriated by the Hong Kong protesters), and gain new meaning from the new space, dependent upon the changing affordances that are offered. As we write this book, platforms like TikTok and Zoom are near their zenith; how might various kinds of visual media be interpreted in these spaces, and how do those interpretations differ from previous ones? By continuing to circulate them, users ensure that these texts stay alive, creating continuity between media forms and perpetuating the evolution of visual cultures.

WHAT ARE THE RULES WHEN IT COMES TO IMAGE COPYRIGHT?

Although it differs somewhat from place to place, we describe here the basic system for image copyright in the United Sates. Depending in part on the special interests involved in its creation, a given image may be used freely if its creator has given explicit permission for it to be part of the "creative commons," (often with a disclaimer such as "you are welcome to use this image but not for profit making") or if it is in the public domain ("this image is available to all free of charge and may be used in any form"). Other images instead have a form of full or restricted copyright ("this image is the exclusive property of a corporation or individual and to use it at all, you must receive permission and perhaps pay a fee or royalties for its use"). Images and moving pictures more than 90 years old are generally in public domain, although in some cases, an image-maker who has made an image of an image—taking a still from a public domain image and putting it in an advertisement, for example—does have a copyright. Likewise, some images more than 90 years old have been carefully re-copyrighted by descendants of the image maker, who hold the inheritance rights to it.

But in circulating copyrighted images, there are some important exceptions to keep in mind. News organizations, and educators, for example, may share images in the interest of informing the public of important events and ideas. Likewise, images are widely used in parody—a satirical art form which exaggerates specific properties of someone or something in order to make a comedic social critique. Parody is actually legal fair use, and creators don't have to pay rights or royalties, or worry about being sued. However, an educator cannot make copies of a copyrighted image to sell for profit, and parody must primarily be in the interest of social critique. Consider, for example, if an advertising agency were to use an image of a popular performer in parodic form for a television commercial in order to sell something; the ad creator and the advertiser would run a high risk of being sued for copyright infringement, because the primary point of the use of the image is commercial sales and not social commentary.

The rules are complex, and everyone from artists to intellectual property lawyers sometimes struggle to keep up with the frantic evolution of technology that makes sharing and manipulating images ever easier.

Exercises

1. Try to capture the same or similar images on a television screen (while watching streaming video, for example), and a tablet or a cell phone screen. Compare the ways the images "feel" to you and ask yourself why there are differences. What about each channel or architecture of the device or media program itself affects the process of viewing? What makes you prefer one type of image or moving picture (video game, movie genre, how-to tutorial, commercial, etc.) on one device versus another? Try to come up with a mini-theory of interpretation about the important ways each particular channel affects your ability to recognize, interpret, and think about an image.

2. Pick an "influencer" whom you like, dislike, or at least know about. Collect about 10–20 images of that person, or images generated by that person. What kinds of image does the person use? Consider both the theme of each image and the type, i.e., selfie, meme, GIF, etc. What was this person's purpose in using those images? Who is their audience, and what about the context of the image would appeal to that audience? Conclude by evaluating how well that influencer understands the visual affordances they are tapping into to use visual persuasion.

3. Visit an online meme generator (there are plenty out there for you to choose from) and create your own meme. Use an image that you think can be pulled out of one context and usefully placed into a new one, with the help of a caption. Post your meme on a social media account and invite a few friends or classmates to create their own versions. Once they have shared their creations, give them just a glance: what catches your eye? What do you notice about how they have taken your original idea and changed it? Do you find their memes funny and/or shareable? What else happens in this experiment?

For Further Exploration

Bolter, Jay David, & Richard Grusin. (1999). *Remediation: Understanding New Media*. Cambridge, MA: MIT Press.

- Bolter and Grusin define remediation and set out their theory of how the tension between immediacy and hypermediacy is one of the process's key elements.

Duchamp, Marcel. (1919 and later). L.H.O.O.Q. Art series.

- Series of experiments in collage and other media around the immense popularity of DaVinci's *Mona Lisa*. This particular series lives on today in new remediations.

Jenkins, Henry, Sam Ford, & Joshua Green. (2013). *Spreadable Media: Creating Value and Meaning in a Network Culture*. New York, NY: NYU Press.

- An examination of how media (not only memes) are replicated and shared in the digital age.

Shifman, Limor. (2014). The cultural logic of photo-based meme genres. *Journal of Visual Culture*, 13(3), 340–358.

- Shifman provides a more nuanced definition of memes by considering how they are related to a culture around digital photography.

7

VISUAL PERSUASION AND POLITICAL LIFE

Introduction

What do we mean by *persuasion*? It is a broad term that refers to how people are influenced in ways ranging from traditional political ideas (e.g., vote for a candidate, support the state in a public works program or demand police reform) to more cultural and social ones (such as a public health intervention to get people to wear masks or avoid shaking hands during the breakout of a transmissible disease). But persuasive influence can also be the effort to get people to acknowledge and accept the existence of an idea, value, or other abstract concept: a religious belief, a widespread notion of what is beautiful. Of course, it can be related to advertising and branding, and in those instances, it involves getting people to identify emotionally and personally with the value of something. Consumers must "buy into" the idea of something before they actually pay money for it. And just as the verb *to persuade* often entails the use of language, in many contexts language itself often relies on our persuasive powers; when we tell stories or report facts, we want the listener to believe the words we're saying. So, in virtually every utterance we make and every image we conjure, we are engaged in some form of persuasive behavior.

Persuasion has a broad scope, and there are different fields of academic study devoted to the various aspects of persuasion, including *pragmatics*, which focuses on particular bits of text and language to analyze how they convey human belief or perception; *rhetoric*, which deals with the broader cultural ideas of persuasive speech and writing; and branches of *psychology* that examine how susceptible individuals are to being persuaded. For our purposes here, we are interested in how images are used for these purposes, in and of themselves, and to support other forms of persuasion. In particular, we see visual persuasion deployed very frequently in the realm of politics, where even the most innocuous message may be carefully crafted to have the maximum impact on the viewer in order to advance a specific agenda.

On Visuality and Persuasion

Roman rhetorician Quintilian pointed out that the best orators create a visual image in their listeners' minds. He noted that once an image is in the mind, it is easy to convince someone that what they have envisioned is more eloquent than the language used to put it there ("a picture is worth a thousand words" even if it took a thousand words to create it!). Beyond words, seeing an image directly has great influence. Visual persuasion has powerful qualities of *immediacy*, the tendency of a medium to obscure its own nature and cause us to feel as though we are present with whatever it represents. (For example, think of children reaching out to try and touch the characters on a TV screen.) You might also think of immediacy as referring to how much something you experience feels like "the real thing" or "being there" in contrast to something that the audience can overtly tell is reproduced, or we might call faked, artificial, or more colloquially, "canned."

Hearing words that relay a story about something that happened in the past involves processing sounds to comprehend them, and then absorbing their meanings. The audience also has to take in the presence of whoever is relaying the story, the acoustic and semiotic qualities of the room or other performance space, the presence of others and what they're communicating, and so forth. Likewise, printed words demand the cognitive effort of reading, and reconciling the text with respect to the other knowledge the reader holds. These kinds of media channels diminish that feeling of immediacy but experiencing an image or moving picture about the same story you have merely read or heard about feels much more like immediately *being there*. Another way to think of the immediacy of image is the way that visual items make us feel as though we are witnessing facts or true happenings. Again, Quintilian illustrated this astutely by describing visual evidence at a trial, where bloodied objects and a prisoner in tattered clothing bring "the cruel facts" of a case vividly to life for those present.

This seeming directness of connection is a major way that images, especially photos and highly "realistic" images (see Chapter 4 on realism as an idea), become **naturalized** to us, meaning that we take them to be part of nature, or how the world simply exists around us. When this happens, we are not inclined to interrogate the truthfulness of what we see; we just accept these things as "natural." This is a very widespread and very powerful form of persuasion. Frequently reproduced and viewed images, in particular, become highly naturalized quickly, so that items like national flags, portraits of saints and reality stars, and advertising symbols and product designs (see box titled *What Is a Mythologist?*) all rely on the naturalized quality of their oft-repeated images to gain our unquestioned loyalty. When we see and accept these objects without question, we also accept the existence of what they stand for, even if we don't consciously acknowledge it. This is very common with things like nationalistic propaganda, religious iconography, celebrity or influencer culture, and mass marketed and branded goods.

WHAT IS A MYTHOLOGIST?

The French scholar Roland Barthes studied how popular arts and design, journalism, nationalism, and advertising came together to influence people from the 1950s onward. He noted that the repetition of images ironically sometimes caused their historical or political meanings to fade away, and instead such images became connected to unquestioned ideas or "truths." One such example is how soap companies started to market the color white to influence buyers of soap, a product that used to come in bricks of dull brown or gray (e.g., take a look at Image 7.2 where you can see a typical color of a bar of soap made before the 1950s).

By the 1950s, chemical engineers were designing soap to appear white due to its associations with "purity." Likewise, concepts like "scrubbing bubbles" as active cleaner were used in advertising campaigns and chemicals were added to detergents to create abundant white foamy lather, until eventually older non-foamy forms of soap became nearly impossible to sell. The association between foam and cleaning power had become naturalized in the minds of consumers to the point that whiteness and foaminess were seen as a necessity for effective cleaning. (To illustrate this, see how many soaps and other cleaning products you can find with or without sodium laureth sulfate, a key foaming agent.)

Over time, whiteness, bubbles and lather came to symbolize health, virtue, and perfection of the teeth, the body, and clothing. Even toothpastes and shampoos came to be designed and marketed with white lathering additives. This marketing has affected generations of consumers of household products and cosmetics as they defined themselves through white products associated with cleaning and beauty regimens. This idea also may consciously or unconsciously connect to aesthetics of race and beauty as well; note that skin bleach is a popular beauty product in many parts of the world. Barthes recommended that critics learn to examine the history and force of myths like "white lather equals cleaning power and purity," many of which are based on visual themes such as images, colors, and shapes. He famously referred to people who critically study the naturalized nature of such images as "mythologists," a reminder that so many of these "truths" that consumers know with certainty are merely the outcome of careful market research and the leveraging of cultural concepts.

The persuasive nature of images is reflected by our very language, which tends to use visual metaphors when describing what we wish to convey: Is that *clear*? Do you *see* what I mean? Have we *shed some light* on this? Can you *picture* what I've been saying? I can't *imagine* what you mean! These common metaphors in speech all suggest that understanding is deeply linked to our perception as being a visual phenomenon. Moreover, for speakers of English (and many other European languages), the idea that understanding involves light, image, and clarity may lead us toward a bias in preferring visual materials as persuasive elements. This connection between vision and mutual understanding is also reflected in the vocabulary of communication and personal experience: *seeing eye to eye, point of view, outlook, eye-opener*, etc. All of these metaphors reinforce the idea that communicating with others, and perhaps with the world, is most effective when engaging with the "mind's eye." Finally, eye contact is considered a very strong form of communication in most culture groups, even when spoken language is minimal; a direct gaze often signifies trustworthiness, and looking away is seen as the mark of a liar. Even young children learn to make or avoid various forms of eye contact with others early in their socialization, although this varies a great deal across cultures. (See Box in Chapter 5 titled *Eye Contact for Individuals and Politicians*.)

Visual aesthetics also have a deep effect on us. Gazing on beautiful and ugly things, whether familiar or unfamiliar, can be used to persuade us to laugh, to love, to become followers of people, to take some kind of action, to attack someone or something, or to walk away from something, and so forth. Famous images involve figures or *figuration*, where the formal and conventionalized repetition of images becomes a special widespread part of the culture. For example, see Image 6.1 in Chapter 6, where da Vinci's *Last Supper*, a figuration of a religious event and a very beautiful painting to look at, is used to satirize online meetings. When we link those figurations to a new thing through *remediation*, they make effective persuasive tools, as exemplified by memes.

Psychology of Persuasion

The visual has both instant and long-term psychological effects on us, a number of which have been scientifically researched, and then adapted into the tools of persuasion. For instance, one curious but important instant visual effect is that the warmer colors like orange, red, and yellow can enhance appetite, which has led to most fast food restaurants decorating or branding their stores with those kinds of colors. Color branding can even reinforce our subconscious connection to products, and certain color tones induce emotions toward brands—one of the reasons why advertisers are very careful to protect their copyrighted claims to the colors associated with their brands.

COLORS AND LOGOS

While logos and slogans have been around for centuries, the outgrowth of marketing as a field of study (mostly from psychology and economics) accelerated in the mid-20th century, in particular after World War II. Consumerism was linked with national pride in the United States and many other capitalist countries at this time. The need to develop punchy, effective branding for the sudden avalanche of products led to the rise of a whole class of illustrators, analysts, and lawyers dedicated to creating and protecting "intellectual property."

The process of designing a logo and other visual elements for a company has only become more complicated over time, especially as the internet has revolutionized how consumers find and purchase items. Even something as simple as choosing a color scheme for a product is complicated by the fact that the printed page and the computer screen have different ways of mixing and presenting color. In the capitalist system, the few players who early and aggressively corner some aspect of the market become the authorities on it—in the case of color, the printing company Pantone stands out as a historical example. Their use of numbers to refer to different hues, and their emphasis on finding combinations of colors that complement each other across media, have made them a heavyweight in the field. It goes to show that even universal concepts like *color* can be commercialized and trademarked. Pantone has further capitalized on this with their "Color of the Year," which they select based on market research and announce to much fanfare. Such is their authority that industries from fashion to web design structure whole campaigns around their annual selection. Pantone's persuasiveness is borne not only out of successful prediction, but also out of their dominance in the field.

Relying on this kind of guidance and the implications, the final design choices can have (at this point, how many websites and social media platforms have copied and tried to capitalize on elements of Facebook's design?), can drive a brand to success. But brands do not only serve to remind and persuade customers of a company's products. They are also shorthand for *all* of a company's practices, and are symbols in every sense—including the semiotic—toward which the viewer can direct all of their thoughts and feelings about a product. A soft drink company logo, the official color of the brand, and social media icon on a webpage each provoke a response, positive or negative, informed by the viewer's personal experience with company advertising, consumption, and knowledge of the company's behavior.

As for long-term effects of visual experiences, events that are frightening, shocking, or otherwise well outside of everyday experience are often associated with trauma. (While this section deals with the visuality of trauma, especially among groups, it is important to note that not all forms of trauma are always visual.) One way of understanding trauma visually is by considering the uncertainties of recovery from traumatic events. People who study these events use the video concept of *replay* to describe the syndrome where we see images in our mind of traumatic moments; trauma may include the dreams and nightmares that refresh such images, creating recurring psychological distress. Such distress might also arise from visual triggers that induce various emotional states, even if they are rather removed from the original experience and can affect both individuals and groups of people.

Moving images and videos have a particularly direct way of both inducing trauma by bringing painful shocking images directly to us, but also in a sense operating like a collective subconscious in which we, as a social group, are subject to the traumatic replay as a mass audience. An early and highly significant example of a moving image capturing such a moment occurred when the Zeppelin company of Germany organized a major press event to promote its airship (or blimp), the *Hindenburg*. Passenger blimps were by far the fastest way to cross the Atlantic Ocean in the 1920s and 1930s, and were admired internationally as the most advanced form of commercial travel. Moreover, Germany and the United Kingdom showcased their national pride and technological prowess by supporting and promoting companies that built these airships. If you look at a detailed picture of the *Hindenburg,* you will see that pressure from the Nazi Minister of Propaganda led to the inclusion of prominent Nazi symbols (e.g., the swastika) and the official *Fraktur* font of the Nazi party on the airship's hull and tail.

But these ships were quite dangerous as they were filled with the extremely unstable and flammable element hydrogen, partly because the United States refused to export other safer elements like helium. On May 6, 1937, the *Hindenburg* was flying over New York City with 97 passengers and crew on a promotional trip, so camera crews were present all over the city and there were many photos made of it moving across the sky. Camera crews were also present at its landing destination, Lakehurst Airbase in New Jersey, just south of New York City. The cruise-ship sized vessel experienced trouble, including a probable hydrogen leak, and during an attempt at landing, the vessel caught fire and exploded. The camera crews who thought they would be filming a routine landing instead captured the exploding blimp in the moments of the crash. The footage was subsequently played over and over in cinemas across the world as a newsreel, the precursor to evening news broadcasts, which were distributed once a week and drew large crowds to attend Saturday movies at the local cinema. Additionally, photographer Sam Shere took a photo of the *Hindenburg* at the moment of explosion that was reproduced in newspapers around the world (Image 7.1).

IMAGE 7.1 Sam Shere's photo of the *Hindenburg* disaster

This disaster, in which 36 people died, was actually not unique—there had been many passenger blimp explosions, and even a deadlier helium blimp crash in bad weather in 1933. The difference with the *Hindenburg* was that the constant international, collective replay of the moving and still images of the disaster traumatized the public, convincing them that blimps were no longer a safe mode of transportation; these massive agents of propaganda became symbols of horror. Suddenly, the era of blimps and zeppelins for commercial travel was over. It wasn't really until the advent of longer-haul, larger-bodied airplanes in the late 1940s that commercial trans-Atlantic crossings by air really came into play.

There are other firsts of visual mass persuasion since the *Hindenburg*. A notable case is the video tape of a Black man named Rodney King being beaten by a group of white police officers in Los Angeles in 1991. Taken with a handheld video camera by a citizen standing on his residential balcony overlooking the street, it was widely circulated on local television news, and as word got out about the spectacular horror of the video tape, more and more news outlets from places other than Los Angeles began to play the footage. With its nationwide, and then partly global circulation, this video had the effect of highlighting Black Americans' experiences of police brutality to the non-Black public. Longer term political effects of this incident were solidified by riots after the circulation of the video, and it was purposefully reproduced at the beginning of Spike Lee's *Malcolm X* film to draw a connection between historical and contemporary events.

Visual Politics and Media Effects

As mentioned above, violent images have a tendency to stick with us and leave a curious kind of traumatic repetition or "replay" of such violence in our minds, like a movie we cannot stop. Images related to even the *threat* of violence, especially lethal violence, also have a powerful effect on human behavior and our perception of the world around us.

Theorists have long noted the "if it bleeds, it leads" principle in the news, by which stories of violent conflict can be used to inflate news ratings. War, crime stories, and ways of dramatizing weapons and war machines are extremely effective ways to agitate or arouse human emotion. This is evident even if you think back on the how human history is represented in storytelling: dramatic poems like the *Iliad*, religious myths about the warriors of the Mahabharata, and bloody stories of beheadings in the Tower of London all continue to capture our imagination and emotions, often to be used for political effect. Media theorists have long noticed that the drama of lethal violence is consciously used in media to create specific emotional effects in viewers. More recently, the *media effects* model, which examines how media operate on our emotions and beliefs systems—often without our complete consciousness of what is happening—has been used to explore how images in social media platforms affect group identification, and eventually political action or affiliation, in some cases.

Generally speaking, there are two kinds of ways images work upon our emotions when it comes to group solidarity:

through *emotional arousal* (an unfortunate term, but the correct technical one for emotional agitation or a heightened emotional response), or through *intellectual appeal* (highlighting ideas for effective action towards a desired social change). Arousal images might create group identification through anger, when certain viewers become angry at the person, objects, or actions portrayed in the image. But some other viewers might also react in the opposite way, experiencing a positive emotional affinity for who or what is being portrayed. In either case, the arousal is greatly heightened when an image has "life or death" qualities. Thus, images of dying or dead people, symbolic images related to death, guns and other weapons, soldiers or police or stereotyped criminal portrayals, all can elicit a media effect that activates ideas of group anger, group fear, and group sympathy, creating a sense of a collective *us versus them* politics.

There are so many examples of this that it is hard to pick the best. As this book goes to press in mid-2020, massive protests were catalyzed by the circulation and political uptake of a horrifying 8-minute video of a white police officer putting his knee on the neck of a Black man who subsequently died of asphyxiation. Likewise, during this same period of time, images have been widely circulated of armed men on the steps of the Michigan state courthouse in the United States, attempting to intimidate local government leaders into dropping enforcement of public safety measures, even as deaths from the COVID-19 virus continued to rise. In their gruesome drama and visuality, the images are almost perfect for social media uptake, and they lead to a seemingly endless repetition of *us versus them* memes at a point of heightened polarization in US politics.

Group Identity, Image, and Protest

On the subject of visuality and protest, researcher Zeynep Tufekci discusses how social media-based movements use images to mobilize people to unite for demonstrations for democracy.

For example, she found that approximately 50 percent of social media posts related to events of the Arab Spring of early 2011 were pictures and videos. One of the most potent illustrations comes from a well-known image that spurred on mobilization for change, that of the burning body of a Tunisian fruit vendor, Mohamed Bouazizi, in January of 2011. This image is widely considered to be the catalyst for the Arab Spring protests that spanned several nations and triggered political change throughout the Arab world, including presidential turnovers in Tunisia and Egypt. After enduring years of underemployment and police harassment as he tried to make a living by operating a fruit cart, Bouazizi spontaneously set himself on fire as a protest against street abuse by the police under the oppressive Tunisian state. A bystander's graphic video of the incident quickly made it into circulation on the internet, and this image served the dual function of both group anger arousal and a sense of group efficacy.

By *efficacy*, we mean that an image's arousal of group affinity using visual symbols can inspire people to believe that collective action is viable and desirable, to the degree that they are willing to join in a political movement. Images of people engaged in political action (including even self-immolation), images of crowds gathering (which symbolizes the power of the collective), images of protest activities like people holding pithy signs with inspiring slogans or pink "pussy" knit hats or rainbow flags, and images of groups holding propagandistic religious or other symbols affect people directly, making them feel that they are connected to a larger movement (whether they are or not). Arab Spring images included many efficacious images of enormous crowds of people marching, bearing slogans and banners with empowering messages, and with women participating in public protest.

Likewise, images of the body of Michael Brown, a young Black man shot and killed by police in St. Louis in 2014, were used for efficacy elicitation in the United States. The sharing of these images on social media was paralleled by the use of Twitter and GIS spotting to orchestrate a dramatic collective demonstration that moved through the suburbs of St. Louis, avoiding police blockades and gathering marchers. This protest went well beyond its immediate geographic area, further expanding and solidifying the Black Lives Matter movement through visual media.

An interesting aspect of efficacy eliciting is how strongly it amplifies the political power of a message in different ways to different people. As mentioned above, five armed white men with semi-automatic rifles on the steps of the Michigan Courthouse, when portrayed pictorially and widely shared, can have immense political uptake across a wide array of groups with very disparate perspectives. To many right-wing viewers, these images portrayed the conservative movement to understand the right to bear arms as a form of personal liberty that also permitted defiance of quarantine restrictions, or conservative ideas that any form of state regulation is anti-American. Meanwhile, memes derived from the same images were used to generate a sense of the hypocrisy of threatening to kill politicians over a killer virus; they were widely shared among liberals as proof that the popular constituencies of the right wing made little sense.

Both the images discussed above lived on well-beyond the immediate context of their effects in Michigan in May of 2020 and St. Louis in August of 2014. The actual circumstances and the individuals involved ultimately mattered not so much as individuals within the media context (although of course any one individual is always profoundly important) but as far-flung symbols that accrued greater persuasive power as they were magnified through circulation. In human hands, so to speak, these images circulated from person to person and were taken up through emotional arousal and efficacy elicitation to affect peoples' personal beliefs and identities. Would you be surprised to know that the number of people in the Michigan demonstrations at the time specified were only in the hundreds? Ultimately, the true circumstances behind each image are harder to know than the new truths that these images are used to build in our social and political lives.

Propaganda and Persuasion

The *Hindenburg* airship had an intense visuality. It was visible for miles, and its logo and other visual markings, including highly publicized images of its luxurious interior, were in part orchestrated by the central Nazi propagandist, Joseph Goebbels. Of course, the airship was a mode of transport, but in fact, all 17 of its voyages from Germany across the Atlantic between either the United States or Brazil were not part of a regular schedule of flights. Rather, they were announced as part of public relations efforts to bring people's minds and hearts to the German state, through amazement or through intimidation. The *Hindenburg* therefore fulfilled the basic function of *propaganda*, a message designed to serve the interests of its producers with no concern for the interests of the receivers. As political propaganda, another way to think of it is as a message in support of the German cause.

Propaganda should be contrasted to the idea of lies, in the sense of misinformation, even though both might be designed to play into the worldview of a particular audience. Lies of course could be *part of* propaganda, but in general, propaganda is a broader term that has more to do with how information, true or not, is used. It is generally related to campaigns or other coordinated multi-level works of publicity designed to achieve mass persuasion of an audience or population. It might be about building support for a potentially unpopular war, or as a tool to soften people to the idea of accepting their own exploitation or the exploitation of others; the *Hindenburg* was about the wonders of technology as much as it was about fomenting acceptance of Germany as a world power.

Not all propaganda comes directly from the state, but it is frequently connected to the state or to national consciousness. Even some advertisements are propagandistic, convincing people that a commercially owned product is a symbol of patriotism or national character. For example, sugary carbonated drinks really cannot be sold in the name of people's self-interest, but only in the interest of the manufacturers and distributors, to echo the definition of propaganda above. Advertisers often use sales pitches for these beverages that intersect with national forms of propaganda in which consuming the beverage is considered a patriotic act or something typical of the national character. Think of beer cans in the United States, for example, that often use red, white, and blue color schemes to signal affiliation with the national flag, and therefore patriotism; "real Americans" drink this or that beer. Likewise, propagandistic advertising as a persuasive exercise to bring people to the aid of the state tends to increase during times of crisis (see Image 7.2 when wartime England seemed to be a great time to sell both the war effort and soap). Lots of

IMAGE 7.2 Patriotic advertisement for soap during World War I, Great Britain, 1915

propaganda, perhaps most of it that we regularly come into contact with, is predominantly visual, drawing on the semiotic and multimodal resources that we have discussed throughout this book, to an end that is not always benevolent.

Misinformation and Fake News

Misinformation refers specifically to creating and crafting information in a deceptive form with the intention of misleading someone. The ability to lie, to dissimulate (to consciously conceal a truth), and the tendency to project our beliefs as a form of truth is part of the creativity that we all use to shape and experience social relations. As highlighted at the beginning of this chapter, the role of vision in the imagination is closely tied to our ability to create misinformation, and "seeing is believing" tends to muddle our ability to be suspicious of what is being projected in front of us. To put that another way, when we see evidence of something we want to believe, we often cannot "override" our first reaction to it, and we tend to accept the item as truthful without question; this is what psychologists call *confirmation bias*. This is easily exploited by propagandists, trolls, and other people who wish to control or affect social relations for their own purposes.

Fake news is exemplary of the appeal to confirmation bias in the 2020s. Lazer et al. (2018) define fake news as "fabricated information that mimics news media content in form but not in organizational process or intent. Fake-news outlets, in turn, lack the news media's editorial norms and processes for ensuring the accuracy and credibility of information. Fake news overlaps with other information disorders, such as misinformation (false or misleading information) and disinformation (false information that is purposely spread to deceive people)." (p. 2).

Fake news can involve using images that are taken out of context, as occurred following the 2013 terrorist bombing of a marathon in Boston; two men who were not suspects were depicted on the cover of a major New York newspaper as the perpetrators of the bombings. (They eventually sued for libel and damages.) Fake news can also involve tampering with images, as when the religiously conservative Israeli newspaper *Hamevaser* digitally edited a photo of a political unity march following the Charlie Hebdo bombings in Paris in January of 2015. The editor removed images of three prominent women politicians who were present at the march, following a conviction that it is immodest to depict women in public in photographs. Both examples are misinformation that involved misdirection and lies in visual form. This kind of misinformation has been around for a long time, but with new technologies and widespread access to them, the sheer volume and velocity of misinformation out there has increased dramatically in the last several years. Besides simply muddying the waters when it comes to knowing about what's going on in the world, it exacerbates political polarization at a rate not seen before, affecting elections, funding for social policies, attitudes towards race and ethnicity, medical decisions that affect individual and public well-being, and other issues of direct consequence in our lives.

Some of the most widespread contemporary forms of misinformation are shared across social media platforms, including *deep fakes*. Deep fakes, in the context of images, are photos and videos manipulated to look valid as real pictures (often involving public figures), but often edited for the purpose of arguing for some conspiracy or other untrue information. In many cases, audio is also remixed or altered to literally put words in people's mouths that they never uttered.

Many of these fakes are put forth by trolls, who set out to anonymously make provocative or deliberately offensive comments in computerized environments. But this sort of trolling can also lend validation to those trying to harm someone as a collective target (someone famous who does something they find offensive, for example), or be used as part of a coordinated campaign against someone or some entity. There are cases of "troll farms," mostly young Eastern Europeans who know how to read and write in various languages, who are hired by foreign agents to create fake news—and in some cases deep fakes—that are intended as political sabotage. They often utilize images grabbed easily off the web, which they then recontextualize in fake news articles, which are posted on what appear to be legitimate news publication sites; these publications, from their website homepages to their articles and to their writers are, also entirely doctored fakes. As with propaganda, the creators' familiarity with how these sites are designed and the semiotic weight of their look and feel, allows them to lull many visitors into a false sense of security, so that they will accept and disseminate the misinformation. This is how fake new catches on and ultimately serves goals like interference in foreign politics or serving specific industries whose works run counter to public well-being.

Image Forensics

We want to close this chapter by pointing out that even as technology is appropriated for unpleasant ends, others work to counter these problems. Computer scientist Giulia Boato is the director of a research group in Trento, Italy that develops approaches to detecting and tracing fake news and deep fakes through multimodal textual analysis. Her group notes that there are so many fakes in circulation that it is not practical to try to search out each and every one manually, so they are developing automated ways to detect the presence of fakes on various web platforms (Lago, Phan, & Boato, 2019). Briefly, both digital splices (when an image is dropped into another image, or erased as in the *Hamevaser* example above) and image recontextualization (when images copied are moved wholescale) leave digital traces that can be detected using algorithms. But that's only part of the story; these fake images are complex in how they construct meaning, and an image alone doesn't quite tell you the motives and ideas behind the new meanings the maliciously altered item intends to spread. Boato and her group also use textual analysis through search engines, natural language processing technologies, and other promising computer science approaches to language and meaning to cross reference altered images with their matching text. The group has achieved some notable success with such approaches.

Work on detecting fake images, especially in the news, has obvious implications for political debate, but also may ultimately have legal implications. If we can trace and expose fake news both as a form of misinformation, but also as a targeted kind of virtual attack, we may begin to develop more sophisticated ways to fight back. Likewise, laws around libel, treason and espionage may need to evolve alongside the technologies that permit new forms of personal and national attack. As our news continues to evolve on the web and across sharing platforms, so will the means to misdirect through evolving forms of propaganda and information sabotage.

Exercises

1. Leni Riefenstahl was a German woman filmmaker whose beautiful films served the Third Reich as propaganda. Pick one of her movies (perhaps *Olympia*, or *Triumph of the Will*) and do a shot by shot analysis of a segment about five minutes in length. What point is she trying to get across in the section you looked at? How did she make specific paradigmatic choices about music, light, sound, actors, and subject to create propaganda about the superiority of the German people? What does she omit in terms of music, light, sound, etc. that would have made the film less propagandistic? After examining Riefenstahl's work, how would you make a propaganda piece today about a subject of your preference?

2. Look for some fake news by searching on the internet for topics that are politically controversial at this moment in time or ask some friends to send you examples that they have encountered recently through social media. How do the images in the fake news sites "work" to either emotionally arouse the viewer or potentially spur them on to action? What images are the most believable and why? What images are clearly fake and how specifically can you tell?

3. With respect and sensitivity, ask some of the people you know who were teens or older in 2001 where they were when the World Trade Center was under attack. Then ask them if they recall specific images they saw at the time and/or the emotions they had around those images. What elements involving those images do their stories have in common? In your opinion, how did images of the World Trade Center towers' collapse create collective trauma?

For Further Exploration

Gorney, Cynthia. (2011). *Machisma: How a Mix of Female Empowerment and Steamy Soap Operas Helped Bring Down Brazil's Fertility Rate. National Geographic Magazine.*

• Short and engaging magazine article that explores the possibility of television soap operas having caused, in part, the demographic crash in Brazil since the 1970s.

Maher, Stephanie. (2015). Interrogating the Wave: Media Representations of Migrant African Youth. Available on the *Youth Circulations*.com website.

• Maher questions the framing of news photos and the ideologies that guide viewers' interpretations of them in the context of refugees arriving on the beaches of Europe.

Rossi, Andrew. (2020). *After Truth: Disinformation and the Cost of Fake News* (documentary). HBO.

* Gripping documentary that explores the real life consequences of fake news.

Zelizer, Barbie. (2010). *About to Die: How News Images Move the Public*. Oxford University Press.

* A fascinating and readable book about how visual news media disproportionately portrays news as something related to hovering between the moments of life and death.

8

VISUAL ENCODING AND DECODING IN THE EARLY 21ST CENTURY

Introduction: Who Are Producers and Consumers of Images?

In this second to last chapter, we tie together several threads of visual meaning-making as it is understood by cultural theorists. How do producers and consumers work together to create dominant ways of seeing, looking, and interpreting visual media? How do they experiment with, resist, and re-craft dominant ways of seeing? So far, we've discussed the cognitive constraints that affect the ways people take in visual information, and we've looked at how the history of visuality, mostly in the West, affects visual meaning-making today. We've also discussed social media and the politics of the use of visual persuasion and propaganda. This chapter moves into the arena of cultural studies and presents a major model by which to understand how images are produced and consumed in systematic way.

Cultural Studies: Encoding and Decoding

Way back in the 1960s and 1970s in England, a group of influential scholars from fields such as sociology, English literature, and economics were beginning to study the influence of mass culture on public and private life. They were responding to rapid social change happening under the influence of things like the relatively new medium of television; tabloid magazines and newspapers; economic life impacted by expanded mass-market advertising and the advent of chain stores; and increased social and ethnic diversity, as people from England's former colonies began to settle on the British Isles in greater numbers, triggering changes in public attitudes toward race, class, and gender. Sociologists and early media and communication scholars were also noticing that mass culture was changing across the Western world as people were obtaining secondary school and university degrees in ever greater numbers. The British public, for example, was being influenced by relatively new forces of social and public identification. Ideas and methods for the study of this new culture were urgently needed. Thus, scholars like Richard Hoggart and Stuart Hall established the Centre for Contemporary Cultural Studies at Birmingham University, and with it, the academic discipline of Cultural Studies. Central to the field is a relatively simple, but very powerful, idea of studying the ways that messages are both *encoded* and *decoded*.

Encoding

Encoding refers to how mass media products and their messages are created and put into circulation. It is not merely about making a message in the moment, but the whole chain of actors, ideas, and influences that go into producing it. Generally, we talk about encoding in terms of mass media like television and popular writing, as well as and advertising, in which the creation of messages is subject to many different conditions and contributors that imbue or "load up" content with specific kinds of meaning. For example, if a major auto manufacturer hires an advertising company to make a streaming content advertisement (ad) to sell a car, that advertising company first gets guidance from the manufacturer on what target markets and sales goals they want the ad to generate. From there, new groups of people enter into the process of creating an advertising message for the auto, as when the advertising agency starts to research demographic data and economic studies on car-buying habits, as well as the psychology of consumer attitudes toward cars and consumer receptivity to different kinds of advertising. Another group of people gets involved in the encoding process when the ad is scripted by ad creatives—people who have traditionally been white urban elites (see box). The director or videographer of the television commercial or streaming content ad is hired and performers are cast. After the ad is made, distributors work on contracts with social media analytics companies to figure out its placement: where and how the ad might best be used both as a streaming media pop-up and across other platforms such as cable television, billboards, and in promotional materials at the dealership or "point of purchase." They will also consider the target audiences and what kind of profiled consumer will see the ad. All of these people and distribution systems encode part of the intended message of the ad according to various related, overlapping, but not identical criteria.

To give a more detailed example from one step in the process, consider casting. Casting—or deciding which actors and images are best for the narrative or message of an ad—is an important part of visual cultural studies. For as people are cast in visual ads and other kinds of mass media, deeper kinds of ideology about who we identify with are put into play, *encoded* into the casting choices. If that auto advertising pop-up is targeting Latinx buyers, then they will have to decide who plays an "ideal" Latinx father in a segment where a new truck is brought home to the family. Writers of ads and casting directors will have to decide how many children he has, and what size and age and body shape they all have. The same goes for his ideal spouse. Should they be dark-skinned or light-skinned Latinx people (however that gets worded in a casting call and depending who applies for the job), and what markers of social class or occupation should their hair, clothing, and shoes portray? What kind of beauty should they have? As you contemplate this, you'll see that there are literally dozens of presumptions about audience identification made by casting directors, all of which affects who is chosen for a carefully crafted family image within the ad (which might look something like Image 8.1).

Decisions like this continue on down the line, until finally decisions about ad placement occur: does this ad come up while playing a shooter game on the iPad that is popular with young Latinx men, or is it broadcast during the evening news on Spanish-language television, which is typically watched by older people? *All* of these choices and decisions about placement and people are part of the encoding process, and once you consider them as a chain of meaning-making, you can see that complete individual control over the meaning of any moving image segment is really an illusion.

Decoding

Encoding is only half the story, because once the consumer of a message receives it, we must grapple with how the conditions for its **decoding** affect its uptake. At first, it seems like a simple idea, that a viewer will decode the message as it was intended. But as we see above, intent is a complex idea and the viewer's idea of the maker's intent is also something imagined, laden with expectations and ideologies. There's great potential for misunderstanding, not unlike what occurs in conversations when someone's intent gets mistaken by the hearer and the message fails to succeed, perhaps causing offense, or even not being understood at all. Cultural studies theorists talk of "preferred

IMAGE 8.1 An "Ideal" Latinx family and their pick-up truck

readings" or "preferred interpretations," or those that strongly correspond to the intentions or goals of the encoded message's creators. To illustrate this, a preferred interpretation for an Army recruiting ad is that a young person sees the ad, and goes to sign up to serve in the army, while a dispreferred reading might be a viewer developing mistrust of the government or the military due to its portrayal of what Army service is like, or what it is for. (We will return to this idea a bit more below.)

There are many ways that decoding can go wrong or right. To continue our example above, we might consider if the pickup truck ad targeting Latinx buyers fell into a timeslot when the ideal buyer was watching television or gaming; perhaps the media company distributing the ad misfired and advertised at the wrong time or to the wrong market segment. (You have probably encountered ads that you found ludicrously off-base from your interests, signaling that you're not the typical target market associated with a particular media environment.) An ad can also misfire based on what rhetorician Kenneth Burke calls *circumference* (did it catch a wide enough market?) and *scope* (does it explain itself adequately to all interested parties?). Often the content of an ads fail because it lacks a wide enough appeal; perhaps it wasn't actually good enough to catch people's eyes or, as sometimes happens, the ad might be very catchy but not actually persuade people to go buy a car or truck. In the case of too wide a circumference, it might accidentally persuade buyers to get a new truck—but from a different manufacturer. Another crucial issue is whether the ad turned off or appealed to a certain segment of buyers in an unanticipated way.

In the complex chain of encoding and decoding messages, there are often surprising outcomes, sometimes positive, but frequently negative, too. Just one misstep in the encoding process—poor product design, faulty market segment research, casting of unlikeable actors, or a script element that somehow turns off buyers—can ultimately change the life story of the products vis-à-vis its consumers. For example, with automobile production and marketing—despite all the various industries' attempts to control market appeal through careful encoding—some products just go wrong in the long run. The Ford Probe (manufactured from 1988 to 1997) was intended by design and marketing to be an affordable sporty car for men between 25 and 55, and it sold very well in Japan and England. But in the enormous US market, the company failed to account for the fact that male buyers were turned off by the first version of the Probe, because they perceived it as a threat to the continued manufacture of the Mustang, a car with mythic qualities to many American men. Fortunately for Ford, they were able to re-encode the car for a new market in order to reduce the "threat" to the Mustang as a quintessential American sports car. They redesigned the Probe under the direction of the first woman car design engineer at a big manufacturer, Mimi Vandermolen. Ford also began a series of marketing firsts, such as placing a full-size photo ad of the car in *Elle Magazine*. The Probe ended up having some sales success in the United States with professional women in the late 1980s and early 1990s, as significant numbers of women were beginning to express their independence through buying cars all on their own (another historic first).

In this example, we are led to important, overarching questions about encoding, decoding, and culture change: do surprising or unpredictable responses to marketing campaigns potentially reflect changing culture for the consumer? Do consumers ever "read against," or as Stuart Hall put it, "oppositionally," to the preferred reading? In fact, consumers sometimes do respond negatively to ads that run quite counter to the intentions encoded by the producers of product and its marketing (as when American men turned against the Probe, deciding its very existence undercut their love of the Mustang). Or perhaps environmental activists might respond to car ads by actively reading against car culture, thinking instead about the social and political problems around traffic, pollution, lack of support for public transportation, and so forth. What is the wider "ecology" of product placement within people's lives, and how does it reflect their beliefs and values?

You can probably see that the process of encoding and decoding is a simple model, but it is full of a series of choices for content creation and content reception that involve a lot of people and a lot of factors. No single actor encodes a complex message like the design of a product, an ad, a television show, a movie, or a political campaign, and no completely unified public consumes those products exactly in the way that the various makers intended. And yet, we do clearly see ways that widely held beliefs and experiences within the culture are reflected in the mass products and mass media that we consume. There is a widespread sense of types and forms in any given national culture that both producers and consumers, encoders and decoders, rely upon to manage the interpretation of meaning making. This is where the concept of hegemony becomes very useful.

Hegemony

The description of the ideal Latinx streaming video ad campaign for a car mentioned above highlights how marketing professionals might imagine the ideal, generic, default Latinx family—father-led, probably heterosexual and cisgender, with a spouse and a few children of a certain idealized type—and the kinds of car they should ideally be persuaded to buy. This was an example of how visual marketing often relies on notions of ideal types in order to sell us goods, but also draws us into a wider social consensus about who people are and who they should be as consumers. It's not just advertising and marketing, and mass media in general that create and maintain these ideas, but they are some of the primary drivers of them.

We keep using the term "ideal" here. In the philosophical sense, we mean the default, "so-normal-we-don't-question-it" ideal, or culturally predominant form that comes to mind when you think of a person or thing. But really, the ideal we mean in this chapter involves the concept of *hegemony*. Be careful when you look up this term—it has a long history in political science—and consider for our purposes here the *cultural* principle of hegemony, which is about the shared consensus or collective idea of what something is supposed to be. Once an idea about how a group of people should behave or identify is widely accepted, to the point that it becomes the default assumption, then it becomes the basis for the exercise of power. A second illustrative example from outside of advertising might help here. There is a widespread hegemonic notion that men who are leaders wear suits or uniforms. Businessmen, politicians, military, police, and firemen all wear fashion items or other gear on a daily basis that creates an automatic reaction for the public: "this guy is in charge and I'd better listen to him."

Hegemony in cultural studies is deeply connected not just to power, but also to social class relations. Those men in suits are leaders within their social class groups; they are the businessmen and politicians who control the economy and our economic relations within it. But also, many uniformed people are highly regarded as the best of blue-collar or working-class people. This kind of visual hegemony is a way that cultural symbols are used to wield *symbolic power* that can translate into material and even physical power through influence over others.

However, people sometimes also have negative responses to the level of power and control held by men in the special outfits mentioned above. People may easily generate *counterhegemonic* responses to men in suits or uniforms, responses that might on some level "talk back" to power. They often do this visually, not verbally. For a while in the early 2000s, many middle- and upper-middle-class schoolboys rebelled by wearing items like kilts or clothing associated with hip-hop culture to school— a direct statement against their fathers' and mothers' social classes. This counterhegemonic dress choice is also an example of a counter-culture practice, where we react to hegemony by manipulating style and visually portraying our rejection of identities associated with hegemonic groups we want to resist. In fact, the reaction to conservative or traditional looks in popular fashion is often the product of youth culture generating new "style."

One thing to not forget about hegemony, though, is that it is often a *subconscious* practice. The same schoolboys who sometimes wear kilts or baggy pants might normally wear school uniforms consisting of suits or button-down shirts with trousers in imitation of the clothing worn by those in power. Putting on this clothing daily and seeing it all around internalizes their sense of belonging to an influential class. They perform their emerging adult class identity through the habitual practices of learning to tie neckties and wear these suits comfortably and unselfconsciously, seeing them on others, developing an appreciation for well-cut cotton shirts, etc. This is how symbolic power is created and operates. The same applies to counterhegemonic power, in which wearing clothing that resists the dominant class, such as punk, goth, or hip-hop clothing, becomes through habit something that one internalizes as a central part of one's self.

There are other pieces to the puzzle of how people create hegemonic power through visual symbolism in clothing. Consider the proposition that men in suits symbolize power. How then does a woman in business or politics dress? Can she get the same kind of automatic respect and attention that a man does if she doesn't visually seem to fit the part? Political consultants are deeply aware of this issue, and women politicians often work double-time to craft a careful image through dress, hairstyles and hair dyes, makeup, and body-type crafting (i.e., working out and staying thin), that somehow tries to project someone simultaneously authoritative (an appearance that indexes or resembles male authority like the "pantsuit"), feminine (sexually appealing to men, or gentle and delicate), and maternal (clothes and physical stances that remind voters of other nurturing women in their lives). This generally means that in order to appeal to the electorate, they must dress within a set of parameters that signify a typical middle-class woman but also displaying some feminine flair—color, jewelry high heels, skirts to the knee (also, consider Supreme Court Justice Ruth Bader Ginsburg who wears a white ruff collar with her judicial robes). Other women politicians sometimes effectively project a personality that downplays traditional femininity through dark colored pantsuits and walking shoes, but even they tend to add jewelry or make up. Meanwhile, male politicians agonize much less over the public presentation of self because they don't really need to; the suit and its clear hegemonic position in our society do the work for them.

The Mainstream and Hegemony

Hegemony is also deeply connected to the notion of the *mainstream*, or the "average" way of seeing things. Mainstream clothing, mainstream hair styles, mainstream music (in whatever form) are all cultural ways that people are bound together to naturalize the consensus that we have shared values (perhaps even when we don't). In many ways, gaining mainstream acceptance of important ideas is actually key to social and political action. Accepting the need for action on climate change, for example, is a developing hegemony; the hope is that soon, the vast majority of people on the planet learn to work together to save all of our futures (see the Box titled "Seeing Climate Change"). Likewise, the counterhegemonic can be progressive or it can be conservative; today's counter-hegemony—the demand for gay marriage in the West, or the demand that women get the right to vote or drive or open bank accounts in more restrictive cultures—is part of tomorrow's mainstream culture.

SEEING CLIMATE CHANGE

Climate change presents a great challenge for encoders and decoders alike. The scientific enormity of the effects of global (and local) pollution, and the almost infinite social and political challenges of coordinating an effective response make it necessary to be selective in how the problems are represented. Data scientists, environmental communicators, governments, and public interest journalists, for example, all use different visual means to educate us and persuade us of the need to act. Many are also responding directly to the counterhegemonic groups that insist climate change is a hoax.

Convincing people that the problem is real can be broken down as a problem of how to best visually portray it. Data scientists have to select variables, often numeric or geographical, and figure out how to balance selectivity with breadth in order to educate lay readers, including science skeptics. Selectively picking a part of the world with less temperature change or sea level rise over time may be part of a fake or misinformation-based news agenda, but comprehensively showing someone a graph with clear colors and simply described variables about temperature, location, and time, for example, can render the broad trends acutely visible. Likewise, a geographic data scientist might show details of accelerated environmental changes through interactive or time-lapse maps that represent rising sea levels (e.g., blue water gradually appears to erode white ice and green land), or changes in agricultural output over the coming century in "breadbasket" and rice-growing regions around the world. The color, movement, time clocks, and animations of these data visualizations can definitely bring a sense of urgency.

Concerned groups and individuals might also choose to present data in infographics. The World Wildlife Foundation, for example, has for years created award-winning infographics to be shared widely. They tend to grab our attention, making us focus on readily understandable consequences of global warming, and something visually appealing often helps the viewer engage with a difficult subject more willingly. Images of polar bears, pandas in trees, and oversized friendly bees with zooming flight lines, are then connected to information bubbles through gorgeous flows of color and layouts that specifically draw the eye in and out of other information, to connect the smaller concepts to the wider issues—polar ice cap loss, deforestation, or the need for sustainable land management.

Note that even people who do not accept the mainstream in their personal lives are at least partly reacting to it. That is, we are almost always either part of the hegemonies or part of a counterhegemonic response to them. However, in some cases, people also face *erasure*, where a great many ideas, images, voices, and even whole peoples (as happens with Indigenous people everywhere) are not encoded into the visual and written record. This is often connected to cultural hegemony, in which those people with the power and ability to encode meaning have such a hegemonic viewpoint—both consciously and subconsciously—that they fail to bring discounted and forgotten people, places, and ideas into systems of meaning. Within cultural studies, this enclosed system of hegemony, counterhegemony, and erasure also is the root of thinks like resistance, many kinds of creativity, and the practice of identity. The next section is only the tip of iceberg, but it provides two examples of how hegemony encodes power, prejudice, and exploitation in internet search engines and ethnic heritage marketing.

Garbage In, Garbage Out

We've already mentioned how marketing ideas often determine visual portrayals that privilege specific points of view. But it is important to address what happens when hegemony is encoded via a complex web of advertising through the social media we share every day. How do commercial search engines that seem to neutrally present us with something we think of as "information" end up shaping public discourse in ways that serve or reinforce the status quo? How does internet-based "direct to consumer" marketing position us as groups with specific (but still carefully constructed and manipulated) consumer identities to whom producers can more easily sell targeted products?

Commercial search engines like Google make their profits partly by consolidating and controlling our access to images, largely for the purpose of drawing us into either commercial websites or direct-to-consumer marketing, as occurs with certain kinds of pop-up ads. (They also collect data from us in the form of images we upload, of course). To do this, programmers create algorithms that run through the internet as though it is a giant database made up of library items, websites, and individual commercial databases, many collected from our own activities, more or less with our permission (so yes, we ourselves are encoding the status quo, in a sense). Each search generates data from both what the algorithm tells it is important, and what materials are already there for the algorithm to look at. Thus, if the creator of the algorithm sees the world in a particular way—and it is important to consider that Google's programming workforce was approximately 70% white male and less than 3% Black as of 2017 and will not have changed radically in the last few years—the algorithm itself will have built-in biases in how it searches and what it finds. Often, the search algorithm will fail to consider the biases it generates through its programming. Add this to the available material out there which already is full of cultural clichés, visual stereotypes, and biases present in the wider culture, and the results can be a recipe for representational disaster.

This is what researcher Safiya Noble found out one day in 2010 when she was searching for fun activities for young relatives, and typed "black girls" into Google. The first site that came up was a fetish porn site. That's when Noble realized that the actual built-in architecture of the internet was engaging in a long history of the sexualization of Black women, and the ways that internet users buy and sell pornography. Google was also recreating (unintentionally, even if irresponsibly) hegemonic structures that construct or situate "black girls" within a particular kind of gaze, while erasing, suppressing, or minimizing more positive portrayals.

The idea of "garbage in, garbage out" refers to the idea that the results you get from a system are only as good as what you have put in. This is instrumental for understanding how we conduct encoding at all levels of our society. For example, a seemingly neutral term like "women" or "girls" entered into a search engine might be combined with other data about us, resulting in algorithms taking the opportunity to try and sell products like make-up, clothing, and lingerie, or alternatively, sites designed to make money from male customers. Seemingly neutral terms like "pretty," "good," or "nice," can also connect us to girls fetishized as beautiful women (perhaps to sell products, or as part of a general trend in world culture to increasingly sexualize children), pornography, and mail-order brides. A study of Indigenous women conducted by one of the authors of this book in 2020 examined the odd combination of inputs and the fetishes that stereotype Native Americans, Aborigines, and First Nations peoples as either mainstream exemplars of beauty, or as alternately as impoverished and forgotten. The images found have captions that ask who is the most beautiful Indigenous woman around, and are juxtaposed unintentionally but poignantly with images of Aboriginal and Native American women and girls suffering from the effects of violence and poverty. There is nothing particularly positive there for an Indigenous girl about herself, and nothing to tell the rest of the world what her stories and experiences are. Obviously, on a wider scale, both racial and gender profiling in visual software and visual images tends to show us that all women must be young, thin, and beautiful.

Marketing Ethnicity and Visual Cultural Appropriation

Images are very easy to take out of one context and rework as commodities, goods, or services, including virtual items that have exchange value in capitalism. Ethnic symbols are especially interesting commodities because they also involve two additional processes: *appropriation* and *fetishization*. Appropriation has complex political implications, but in action, it simply refers to lifting or stealing an image, song, type of dress, hairstyle, etc., from a nonmajority or nondominant ethnic group, particularly without seeking honest permission or giving credit to the creators. Fetishization is a more slippery concept, but it is a form of appropriation by the majority which personally invests in ideas that essentialize ideas of culture about the people from whom the item was taken; another way of saying this is that an appropriated item becomes fetishized when it its special value to the mainstream is based on an exoticized ideals.

Anthropologist Richard Rogers has studied how the "Kokopelli" image (a silhouette of a dancing flute player with feather-like protrusions on his head) has been appropriated from Southwest Native American rock art and become a symbolic form for working out the tensions of masculinity experienced by Euro-American men. The origins and prehistory of the image come from ancient Anasazi rock art, which is popularly shown to non-Native American tourists who visit the Southwest United States. Additionally, there are more recent Hopi visual traditions that feature insects with feelers and proboscises (namely, cicadas and robber flies); in the agricultural past, these may have been fertility symbols, since insects are associated with agricultural production, while proboscises and the flutes they resemble are associated with male reproductive organs. However, in the late 1980s, these images were taken, altered, given a poorly translated name and commodified as the contemporary cartoonish figure of "Kokopelli." Since then, these reworked images are used for non–Native American corporate logos, tourism promotion, and images in commodities ranging from jewelry to bathroom sets sold at big chain stores. It has also been the subject of dozens of fetishistic websites for mainstream consumers to learn about the primitive and noble "other"—a problematic stereotype that reflects new forms of exoticizing Native Americans as ideas or objects, rather than people with a specific and brutal colonial history under Western dominance.

Image commoditization means taking an image from a specific and meaningful context and fetishizing it in a new context in a way that speaks to its new audience. Kokopelli certainly didn't symbolize to the ancient Anasazi people, or for that matter contemporary Hopi people, a dreadlocked musician who rides mountain bikes, skateboards, plays guitar, and seduces women in the model of a rock star on a road tour. And yet, those are all ways that appropriated and fetishized Kokopelli images are deployed to appeal to non–Native American men's inner dudes. The prehistoric Native American images have been changed from insect to human, religious artwork to cartoon, and ancient fertility symbol to a figure that represents modern (mostly) white men's anxiety over their masculinity, sexuality, and freedom in a corporate culture where they must answer to the boss or to their wives. This kind of abstraction allows a once Native American image to become part of economic exchange in mainstream culture in the United States, and perhaps worldwide (see Brazilian example in Image 8.2), where its vague connotation of "Indianness" enhances its supposed desirability as something "different."

IMAGE 8.2 "Indian" headdresses as party accessory, Rio de Janeiro

Ultimately, this fetishization of ideas about colonized peoples often turns appropriated images into empty ciphers. These ciphers are ready-made containers into which anxieties are dumped and used for catharsis or generally working through social tensions. Most mainstream images and ideas about non-hegemonic groups are really all about the tensions within the mainstream culture, offering distorted images and concepts to an audience that decodes them, almost magically and very ironically, into something "authentic" in a world where all images seem subject to the emptiness that comes with commoditization.

Visuality and Identity on the Internet

This chapter has so far discussed the basic ideas of encoding and decoding, and notions of hegemony. There are other models, however, of how to understand image production and interpretation, especially with the advent of television, video, and various forms of online content. In particular, when we stop operating in a traditional face-to-face mode, we start to experience identity and practice our identities, and respond to the symbolic identities of others in changing ways.

Probably one of the biggest changes across generations involves the advent of *context collapse*. Context collapse occurs when someone broadcasts to an unseen audience; doing this erodes the boundaries between the different groups to whom you'd present different selves, leading you to present a "lowest common denominator" self, palatable to everyone (because the audience could be anyone). This effect of not being able to fully utilize the context of your communication to shape your message and not being able to display a context specific personal identity has had a profound impact on how we use social media, and interesting effects on the self-presentation of webcasters, especially in D.I.Y. environments. Another effect of context collapse is that the speaker becomes hyper-aware of the self as a stand-alone individual because in a sense, under the conditions of context collapse when there is no discernible audience to respond to, the self is all that there is! Hyper-consciousness, new forms of self-consciousness, and how our awareness of both changes over time is a big topic, some of it covered in Chapter Two of this book. For our purposes here, we will specifically address how people try to grasp the introduction of new visual technologies affects the sense of individual and collective identities.

Interestingly, sociologists, media theorists, and visual anthropologists have noticed for more than 120 years that self-consciousness is altered through photographic technology. They have documented examples of how individuals and groups within many societies and cultures have revised their general attitudes toward the idea of the self after the introduction of photography and video. Many cases from around the world show that the presence of popular media portraying everyday lives gives audiences new forms of self-identification and individuality. This can be seen with melodramas broadcast by Egyptian television in the 1980s, in which ordinary working women saw themselves in abstract television characters, and utilized emotional identification as a new form of self-expression. Likewise, a documentary team of Kayapo indigenous people learned from a Brazilian film crew how to create visual content for a political campaign to draw attention to the destruction that would be wrought on their lands with the construction of a hydroelectric dam. As Kayapo filmmakers and their entire communities started to imagine themselves in new social contexts (including a filmic, or digital, context), they further developed their own indigenous sense of community politics and action. They engaged in novel political activities in a distinctly Kayapo voice and manner; contrast this story with the "Kokopelli" appropriations above, where indigenous encoders are left entirely out of the picture.

Since the late 1990s, digital environments have led to new forms of self-making and identity practices. For example, stark differences have emerged between women's and men's use of visuality on the web and in other visual media. Reflecting earlier trends, but building on them through social media, women's visual culture on the internet often includes fashion marketing that also deals with ideas of emotional management, expressions of self-branding, and demonstrating "effortless perfection" in virtual form.

SHOOTER GAMES, THE MILITARY-ENTERTAINMENT COMPLEX AND MASCULINITY

Shooting has been a part of digital games since the beginning of the medium. *Spacewar*, widely considered the first digital game, was developed by Stephen Russell at the Massachusetts Institute of Technology (MIT) in 1962 on a computer "larger than many automobiles, but tiny in comparison with many of the computers of the time" (Wolf, 2001). *Spacewar* featured space combat for two players, one of which controlled a wedge-shaped spaceship, while the other controlled a cigar-shaped ship. In the middle of the screen there was a sun that provided gravity allowing the players to move. The ultimate goal of the game was to destroy the ship of your opponent. The action of shooting was easy to understand, and with the limited technology available, animating a single pixel floating from one player's ship across the screen to interact with another player's ship was a relatively simple proposition. This has since led to a proliferation of shooting as possibly the most common action overall that players take in digital games, despite the fact that there are only so many ways that games that can recreate ping-pong.

So, shooting has, at some level, been encoded into digital games from their beginning. Digital games are products of the military-industrial complex of post-World War II America—the "military-entertainment" complex (Kline, Dyer-Witheford & De Peuter, 2003)—and are artifacts historically rooted in a specific time and context, the heightened fears, and the unprecedented military buildup of the Cold War. According to Kline et al., this has created a "cultural channel or groove" of militarized masculinity in the digital games and the game industry. In digital games, as pixel counts have gotten higher, and resolutions sharper, shooting has not only proliferated, but thrived as the mainstream, hegemonic interaction in the industry-leading, big-budget, AAA games. According to NPD Group, over the last decade (2010–2019), the top selling game every year featured shooting as a primary mechanic. The most popular game in 7 of those 10 years was an entry in Activision's *Call of Duty* franchise (Morris, 2020). In short: violence sells.

It is important to remember who this violence is being encoded for and decoded by. Men, particularly young, white men, are more likely to work in the digital games industry (Weststar, Legault, Gosse, & O'Meara, 2016), be represented in digital games (Williams, Martins, Consalvo, & Ivory, 2009), and are more likely than women to play digital games (Lenhart, Jones and Macgill, 2008). This leads to a cycle of encoding and decoding where old ideas are consistently perpetuated by games publishers, designers, and developers who have been shaped by that very same groove. This leaves out more differentiated types of game-play (i.e., not involving shooting guns), as well as diverse viewpoints and minorities in terms of story and character. The dominance of shooter games therefore illustrates the power of the mainstream to replicate itself through com-plex industrial practices of encoding and decoding.

For example, young women in the fashion industry consciously pursue ways to create a visual self that stays ahead of, and even defines, contemporary aesthetic ideas of fashion and ideal wom-en's bodies, especially in how they appear as bodies in social media. Often, they labor tirelessly to maximize the appeal of their outward appearance through forms of self-discipline and self-modification, such as regulating diet or undergoing plastic surgery, paired with networking and the crafting of a primarily visual persona that nonetheless is meant to relate to others as a "real" person. In and of itself, this is a kind of emotional regard for self that tries to make the avatar into the person, rather than the person informing the avatar. Although these actors may be motivated by trying to break into the fashion industry or lucra-tive promotional contracts as influencers, whether one becomes a professional model, a social media influencer, or is merely an adolescent girl profoundly influenced by how beauty culture is constructed online, the sense of gender identity is a primary way of encoding both being and image for many.

Conclusion: The Future of Encoding and Decoding in Influencer Culture

This chapter wouldn't be complete without a few notes on what encoding and decoding will look like in the future as individual content creation and mass media environments change. Notably, micro-visual items like selfies, street photography, and short video pieces are becoming increasingly important forms of influencer and brand building. Mass marketing once put much of the control for content creation into the hands of the (mostly white, mostly male) big advertising firms, Hollywood, and television networks, and they were the particular funnels through which encoded images and meanings were shared with vast numbers of the population. Today, audiences and channels are greatly diversified and traditional mass advertising tends to reach only older cable TV and news audiences. Meanwhile, by using social media as a novel form of mass communication, content creators can be both influencers and their followers.

There are still some of the older tensions in which the counterhegemonic and the hegemonic have interplay within new media. Micro-influencers, who are generally those who are trying to get brand deals and trying to monetize their web presence, tend to have better campaign engagement with their followers—that is, they are well-trusted by followers who respond directly to them either through expressions of loyalty or through responses to direct sales offers. This level of strong identification means that micro-influencers can gain contracts with big agencies to promote various brands relatively easily, and yet there is a catch. When people become macro-influencers, their reach becomes bigger and they have more resources as they successfully monetize their personas, gaining lots of lucrative contracts. But their influence strength will decrease as they become more celebrity-like and people start to trust them less—their audience is starting to decode them as perhaps too hegemonic (i.e., so mainstream that they've lost their edge) or maybe too far removed in the sense of friendship networks to be trustworthy.

It's not totally clear where mass advertising will evolve with this new paradigm centered on brand influencers, or where and how encoding and decoding will continue to change when it comes to the mass circulation of image. Nevertheless, we can be sure that those twinned processes will remain an essential framework for understanding how visual messaging is being produced and consumed, and therefore crucial for being a careful reader of the ever-increasing amount of data around us.

Exercises

1. Make a list of YouTube celebrities or influencers. How do these content creators encode hegemonic ideas in some of their work? If they use counterhegemonic creative efforts, what are they, and what are they speaking back to? How do the tensions between the forms of hegemony work as a creative for that you, as a decoder, can detect and interpret?

2. What do missteps in advertising look like? Find a couple of examples of advertising you have received via social media or other channels that have seemed really "off the mark." Who do you think the advertiser was trying to appeal to (age, gender, location, and other demographics)? Can you come up with a possible explanation for why you were incorrectly targeted for these ads?

3. Review the discussion on dress codes and schoolchildren internalizing a sense of social class belonging or authority through dress habits. Does it always work in the manner described above? What do school uniforms do for or with working class children, who may or may not grow up to be part of the suit wearing or uniform wearing class? Do they nonetheless internalize something about looking the part, or who deserves respect based on visual cues through

dress? What kinds of counterhegemonic dress are possible with school dress codes? Does any of this reflect on gender politics in classrooms or the wider world?

For Further Exploration

Goffman, Erving. (1979). *Gender Advertisements*. New York, NY: Harper and Row.

• Precise and fascinating guide to how gender differences are established visually within advertising.

Hebdige, Dick. (1979). *Subculture: The Meaning of Style*. London, UK: Routledge.

• Groundbreaking, now classic, study of how youth style is an expression against the mainstream, a "symbolic resistance."

Nixon, Sean, Stuart Hall, & Jessica Evans. (Eds.). (1997). *Representation: Cultural representations and signifying practices*. London, UK: Sage Publications.

• Case studies in advertising, magazines and sports of how race and gender hegemonies are created. Great visual illustrations.

Noble, Safiya. (2018). *Algorithms of Oppression: How Search Engines Reinforce Racism*. New York, NY: New York University Press.

• After writing this book, Noble was hired by Google to make suggestions on how to rebalance their algorithms to provide more balanced forms of representation internet searches.

9

VISION, TECHNOLOGY, AND THE FUTURE

Introduction

We've stressed in the previous few chapters the growing importance and presence of visuality in people's lives, especially with the increased availability of visual technologies such as streaming video, smart phones, and internet platforms that encourage us to share images. We've also looked at how visual technology and the ability to recontextualize images and words in new digital environments can facilitate both the generation of fake news and the formation of internet-based social movements. And we've talked a bit about visuality in relation to consumer marketing forms in social media and online stores. Overall, we've emphasized visuality and culture in general, and how the ways these images make meaning reflect our sense of self and social action within society. Human behavior has always been tied up with our capacity to generate and interpret images, and human history is both deeply reflected within and created through visual means. But what about the future? This chapter engages with futurology, or the projection of what the future of vision, visuals, and visuality could look like based on our understanding of current trends.

Futurology

Americans have a well-deserved reputation for thinking that a better future is achievable through technology. This "techno-utopianism" fuels research and development, markets and capital investments, medicine and transportation, and all of the social and emotional life that surrounds these things. Even while this utopianism blossoms from our sense of having an enhanced quality of life, or that technology itself is life-giving and life-extending, our rosy view of the values of technology can blind us to how it also creates (many) problems in unforeseen ways.

Unsurprisingly, the United States and Japan—another country well-known for embracing the cutting edge of technology—are often seen as leaders in the aesthetics and design of media and objects that index "the future" worldwide. Their inventions, visual arts, and products quickly reverberate around the world, providing ever new opportunities for visual culture and new forms of visuality to expand in public and private experience. Video, image enhancement technologies and the software that brings visuality to us from these countries (and others, of course) are part of new applications and new technologies developed on a daily basis. The pace of development is also accelerating all the time, almost exponentially. Here's just a short list of some visuality-related devices and advances over the past century that have significantly changed our idea of the limits of *what we can see*: diagnostic imaging like X-ray machines and MRIs, miniature cameras, microscopes that can see down to the subatomic level, satellite images (whether of Earth or of deep space), military targeting cameras on drones, the most recent display and projection technologies, digital photo editors, internet video chat, light sculpting technologies like holography, image-based social media, facial recognition software and surveillance, body cameras, virtual and augmented reality headsets, neural networks that can sort intelligently through visual data of all kinds, and much more. At the same time, science fiction authors, advertisers, and political lobbyists (to name a few groups) have all continually updated their ideas of what the coming decades or centuries might look like, incorporating these developments and more. What we envision as "the future" in changes to accommodate the new, as well as what is still on the horizon.

Many of these items have been motivated by the needs of, and developed with the financial backing of, the military and government, but others are the products of safety laboratories, medical research, internet and software companies, artists and designers, and entertainment industry specialists. This makes many of them hegemonic in their conception, application, and distribution, and indeed, there is a kind of digital divide between creators and consumers, nations and regions with big tech economies, and nations and regions where citizens have limited access to both the social and quality-of-life advantages of such technologies.

Some visuality-based technologies seem exotic at first and are very splashy immediately with consumers: cell phones with cameras appeared in 2002, when Nokia introduced a mobile phone with its own camera, featuring color images and 178x206 pixels. By 2006, camera phones surpassed sales of *both* digital and film cameras, which had been the only photographic options for the previous generation. Others may seem a bit silly or "gimmicky," like refrigerators with smart screens (although this is arguably a step up from alphabet magnets). Commentators often talk about the "Internet of Things" as the future of consumerism, where everything from doorbells to dishwashers can be connected to the home Wi-Fi. Given that so much of our interaction with the digital is based upon the visual—you can't exactly see the electromagnetic waves that are enabling your device to be "smart"—these novelty items rely on affordances like touchscreens and LED lights. This is a semiotic process like anything else, where the form of the object, or what we can see of it, at any rate, is a kind of sign that creates a sense of futurity.

It's also important to note that many visual technologies become mundane quickly (do you know anyone without a cell phone camera today?), and new life-saving applications are often developed from vision technology originally made for other purposes. That is, beyond our being mesmerized by the technology of the moment, members of our culture value these technologies because we believe they will have other applications in other arenas in the future. For example, everyone from plumbers to civil engineers to scientists have recognized and developed the value of small remote imaging technologies for projects like mapping what's going on underground, or unlocking more information about cellular and molecular processes. Tiny cameras are used more and more commonly for minimally invasive microsurgeries, while biomedical engineers try to patent new procedures partly dependent on visualization, and vision-enhancement technologies, such as LASIK or optic implants. And of course, there are "miracle" procedures that restore or clarify human vision, which in turn affect the culture of visuality and the discourse surrounding vision.

It's impossible to predict the future in most instances, but it's not always folly to try to imagine what it might look like. We conclude this book by with a bit about the futurology of visuality or forecasting what visuality will be like in the future based on trends and trajectories we see today. We focus upon three general trends—augmented reality, observational astronomy, and facial recognition—but the number of options is countless and growing all the time.

Augmented Reality

A term for our era commonly heard today is the "post-human." *Post-humanism* as a philosophy has many pieces, but is especially focused on how since the Enlightenment era, our human-centeredness seems to be giving way to a future where what we once understood as under human control and part of human consciousness has shifted. Some of this is derived from the development of biological procedures like cloning or assistive reproductive technology, wherein babies no longer have to be conceived and born the "traditional" way, or environmentalist theories that the planet is rising up to counter our hubris about pollution and fossil fuel use. But much of posthumanism also stems from acts of imagination that place humans in new interactive environments with very large (or very small, but either way always present) machines, often for the purpose of enhancing their perception, or experience, of the world (Image 9.1).

IMAGE 9.1 An interactive exhibit at Indonesia's Museum of Augmented Reality; note the virtual object that the visitor's onscreen avatar is holding

Computer-based interaction is based partly on the vision and visual culture of humans. It might feature things like three-dimensional television and gaming systems, computerized interactive sex programs, interactive goggles or other wearables, the list could go on for a while. These are often imagined both as products and as science fiction—*Star Trek* holodeck, anyone?—and the two tend to inform each other. Perhaps you've already experienced one of these through an *augmented reality* (or "AR") app on your phone? Such apps are used as mobile devices that travel with you in the real world, screens on, adding characters, figures, colors, sounds, and even narratives to the actual visual environment. Used most notably in treasure hunt and/or battling-for-territory apps like the game *Pokémon Go*, the experience of augmented reality makes players feel like they are interacting with a richer environment than they usually do, perhaps even imagining the world to be full of magical creatures once hidden from us and now rendered visible. Products based on this sort of overlay visual technology are being developed almost daily, from the lines of scrimmage that magically appear in football broadcasts, to the designer overlay scenes that generate excitement on home improvement shows.

Augmented reality is contrasted with *virtual reality*, which creates visual environments out of nothing, rather than overlaying images on what already exists. But we haven't quite reached the point where VR is as widespread and convincing as we imagine it should be, that is, able to fool us into thinking it *is* reality. As with other forms of remediation, it is AR's blending of immediacy and hypermediacy that probably makes it so thrilling—especially when what is being remediated is the very world around you, which you are still aware of. It remains to be seen if this thrill will die down as augmented reality applications become a greater part of our everyday movement through space. If it does, we predict that another new thrilling form of hypermediacy will come along, so that we can continue to push the boundaries of our perception.

MAP TECHNOLOGIES AND AUGMENTED REALITY

The word "augment" implies something better than the way things were, and it's debatable whether all the technologies we're currently swimming in make our lives easier, or give us more information about the world. Yet in a very broad sense, one technology that has been directly changing our understanding for thousands of years, and continually improving, is mapmaking. It may seem strange to talk about a piece of paper with lines and figures on it as an AR technology, but think about it: they remediate your experience of space in a very direct way. The range of human vision is only a handful of kilometers in optimal conditions, more if you happen to be on a mountain or an exceptionally flat part of the globe. The diligence of traders and explorers over the centuries has enabled ever more accurate maps to be created, so that we can conceive of states and nations far larger than what we could see for ourselves. (When we talked about spatial modes in Chapter 5, this is one example of how they can be modified by media.)

These days, it seems like hardly anyone uses paper maps to navigate anymore, since smartphones and car-based GPS are so ubiquitous, and user-friendly. As we alluded to in Chapter 2, this has remediated the experience of space again: in your pocket, you probably have a device that will allow you to navigate an unknown place with a minimum of fuss, meaning that place will not remain unknown for long. Not only that, but different apps allow you to check traffic, find restaurants, or even search for romantic partners, giving you much more information about your surroundings than you could readily locate with your eyes. Not everyone will derive equal benefits from all these, but much as the

nautical charts and road maps of past centuries continually improved, this stream of technology has remained a
popular target for updates. For better or for worse, they
change what we think about different places, what they
contain and how they are divided; and as with so many
other advancements, it is an open question whether they
will draw us together or push us apart.

Surveillance and Law Enforcement

In June of 2020, Detroit police arrested a middle-aged Black
man based entirely on analysis of closed circuit television
(CCTV) video surveillance of a thief at a downtown mall.
Using facial recognition software, an algorithm was the only
thing the police department used to identify a man named
Williams who was believed to have stolen some watches. It
turned out that Williams was nowhere near the location of the
theft when it occurred, and this false arrest incident entered
the public record as one more example of police overreach and
unlawful arrest and detention. In fact, almost immediately after
the incident, the Detroit police had to announce a new policy
that facial recognition technologies could only be used to help
identify suspects *in conjunction with* traditional policing modes
such as collecting witness statements, establishing alibis, finding
clues at the scene of the crime, and so forth.

Well beyond the implications for racism in policing—
although it is crucial to note that algorithmic bias in facial recognition programming consistently mis-identifies people with
darker skin—this incident captured national attention because
it is emblematic of the many frightening possible outcomes
of widespread video surveillance (and other practices such as
mobile phone tracking). For example, besides the possibility
that falsified or simply incorrect video evidence could lead to

someone being wrongly prosecuted for a crime, surveillance has already been shown to be used selectively for biased execution of law enforcement or entrapment. The American Civil Liberties Union (ACLU) warns that the government or law enforcement often claim that cameras are installed to monitor public space against the acts of terrorists, yet again and again, such camera technology is used mostly to facilitate petty crime arrests. Likewise, many studies have demonstrated that the presence of cameras does not actually reduce crime or reduce the public's fear of crime. Cameras installed as hardware in an environment tend to become a naturalized element in that environment, and we simply stop seeing them after a while (even if they don't stop seeing us). It should be noted, however, that law enforcement and civil liberties experts do agree that video surveillance, including facial recognition software applied against terrorism, is a valuable tool if correctly placed, monitored, and consistently used primarily for the purpose intended; think of its use in train stations, airports, and government buildings.

There are additional ways that these visual surveillance technologies are starting to play out for the future. As with other technologies (remember, the future is usually seen as a utopia), it is easy to suggest a technology fix for policing bias: the body cam. The idea is that police officers will be better practitioners of the use of force—and more easily exonerated when it is used—if digital computer video from body cameras is available to record officers' actions. In practice, they tend to get shut off, fall off, get moved sideways, record poor or partial images, or are otherwise tampered with; they have proven to be very limited or very selective in either regulating police behavior or recording incidents in a way useful for resolving the truth of violent incidents. Currently, too, some people are proposing these cameras be used for surveillance and suspect identification, raising some of the possible problems mentioned above.

Part and parcel of surveillance is facial recognition. This technology has a more uncertain future in a sense, as it's shown itself to be deeply vulnerable to the "garbage in, garbage out" idea. Facial recognition can be used to invade privacy, and if you consider that social media and smart phone software might analyze face data in your photos and feeds, this may become a more serious issue in the future than we are ready for.

When facial recognition is used with policing, as the Williams story demonstrates, it may be unconstitutional or downright sinister—so sinister that the massive technology company IBM stated it will no longer develop generalized facial technology software of the kind which is currently used in policing. (Note that facial recognition used to match particular individuals to databases, as occurs with smart phone logins or for passport control at airports, is a different system and is still widely expanding.) Facial recognition is nonetheless used in about 25% of police departments as of 2020 as an aid for criminal investigations, with all the potential pitfalls that entails.

Techno-Utopianism Is Also Dystopianism

We hope that the descriptions above show how "Big Brother" is actually a mundane but very real problem in daily application with surveillance by security forces. The idea of a society where the individual is made powerless by total surveillance was part of prison technology in the 19th century, and was later brought later into general popular consciousness through the novel *1984*, by George Orwell. Orwell's 1948 novel is about a dystopian society in which the population is monitored by an all seeing, technology-aided leader, and it brings home even for today's reader the problem of how technologies of surveillance are tempting tools of control for authoritarian leaders and their allies. In fact, the general scariness of surveillance is always present around fears for the future, motivating a lot of political and social movements that question uses of technology. We use the word "Orwellian" to negatively describe this kind of situation, which grows less hypothetical every year; more recently, media like the streaming series *Black Mirror* capitalize on these concerns.

It isn't only governments who seek to take advantage of this technology and mentality, either. In many city neighborhoods, miniature and/or hidden cameras are used even by residents for home security (see Image 9.2). While it may seem perfectly reasonable to want to protect your own property, there is growing evidence that some instead use these devices to monitor their area for what they see as undesirable elements (read: ethnic minorities, homeless, and/or youths). Neighborhood social networks like Nextdoor have had to explicitly warn users about using racialized descriptions of people they've seen on camera who they suspect of crimes, as all too often, this sort of citizen policing is what leads to, for example, the tragic deaths of unarmed young Black men. The idea of everyone policing each other, besides the echoes of Cold

IMAGE 9.2 A typical notice of surveillance in a residential neighborhood

War-era secret policing, is related to the idea of the Panopticon, derived from the Greek for "all-seeing." In its original conception by the philosopher Jeremy Bentham, this was a prison design where all the cells faced a central, 360-degree guard tower, so that the guards could look into any of the cells at will; the idea was that the prisoners would be on their best behavior, in case the guards might be watching. French philosopher Michel Foucault expanded this idea to talk about society as a whole, where neighbors keep an eye on neighbors in the belief that this will cause everyone to be a "model citizen." The problem, of course, occurs when different people have wildly different ideas of who a model citizen is, and are often at odds with the actual laws that dictate how people must behave (and the punishments they receive if they don't).

Nevertheless, the technology is here, probably to stay. If we have to live with, we ought to know whose images are being captured, by whom and how, what those images portray, and what the real-world consequences are, in order to understand the cultural effects of surveillance. Do also keep in mind some of the more contemporary benign applications (that may or may not also seem scary to you), as with smart phones that can leverage face recognition technology to "see" and welcome in their owners, and the US Department of State's combination of facial recognition and fingerprint data to expedite the movement of "trusted travelers" (yes, that's the technical term for those of us who register our passports with biometric data) through immigration and customs at the borders. Anything benign can quickly turn sinister, but we also have the power to help change the sinister into the benign if we, as actors within our culture, cultivate awareness of and care for what the future of visuality might look like.

Observational Astronomy

It isn't unreasonable to say that astronomy is the oldest science in the modern way we understand the term. Humans have been gazing upwards since—well, probably since the beginning of the species. But importantly, we have been observing their movements, recording their positions, and recognizing the cyclic nature of the Sun and Moon, stars, planets, and other heavenly bodies. The transmission of this knowledge predates even writing, as ancient monuments like Stonehenge in England were constructed and aligned with astronomical patterns thousands of years earlier. In relation to visuality, most cultures around the world have divided the night sky into constellations, making maps through generations of storytelling. While people relied on religious or convoluted philosophical explanations for why the stars appear and move the way they do, and the separation of astrology from astronomy is fairly recent, the heavens have remained an attraction to the eye for all these millennia.

We spoke in Chapters 2 and 3, about the science of optics and the development of perspective in the Renaissance, two elements that found their way into astronomy with the development of the telescope. Famously, Galileo Galilei pointed one at the stars in the early 17th century, observing for the first time the moons of Jupiter and the rings of Saturn. It became clear that there was much more going on up above than could be seen by the naked eye—a notion that met with a great deal of resistance at the start (at least in Europe), as the Church felt threatened by these new, nonreligious ideas of how the universe functioned. But with the accelerating pace of scientific study through the Enlightenment and the Industrial Revolution, right into the 20th century, our thirst for knowledge won out. As telescopes became more powerful, and especially with the invention of photography to better record astronomers' findings, we better equipped ourselves to understand the large-scale structure of our Solar System, our galaxy, and beyond. In turn, this informed our perspectives on gravity, quantum mechanics, and many other scientific concepts, eventually enabling us not only to catalogue the stars, but send rockets, satellites, and even astronauts there.

Obviously, not everyone is cut out to be an astronomer. Like any other scientific profession, it requires years of careful study and training to continue the progress that humans have made over the centuries. But the mystique of seeing a planet up-close for the first time, or a colorful photo of a distant nebula, remains undiminished. The Hubble Space Telescope, although plagued by errors when it was first launched, has for decades provided dazzling images. Space agencies like NASA or the ESA often promote their missions with photographs, knowing that although the technical data might be more valuable to them, the public will find "firsts" more appealing: first photo from the surface of Mars, first close-up photo of Pluto's surface (whose heart-shaped Tombaugh Planitia provided endless meme fodder in 2015), first image of a black hole. Perhaps the most famous of these is the "Blue Marble" photo of the Earth (see Image 9.3), taken by the crew of Apollo 17 in 1972 as they traveled to the Moon. It has become a visual shorthand for the idea of space, the audacity of humanity in traveling to the stars, and the way we are unified by all living on one globe.

There are other branches of the field that may be more important to scientific progress than this one, called "optical" astronomy because of its relationship to visible light. Astronomers often make observations with instruments that detect other wavelengths of radiation, such as the infrared and the ultraviolet—but these usually make for less impressive images in the public eye. Other astronomers are concerned with recording radio signals (such as those involved with SETI, the Search for Extra-Terrestrial Intelligence) or continuing to develop theories about physics from existing records. Still, there are sometimes surprising moments of crossover between the professional and the casual. For example, the makers of the science fiction film *Interstellar* (being part of a medium and genre that has capitalized extensively on the visuals of outer space) hired astrophysicist Kip Thorne as a science consultant; one of his jobs was to ensure the accuracy of how the filmmakers depicted a black hole central to

IMAGE 9.3 The Blue Marble, probably the most famous and most culturally iconic photo ever taken of the Earth from space

the film's plot. Thorne provided the effects team with calculations that they used to create new software to render the images, but all involved were surprised at the outcome, while moviegoers were (presumably) awed by the complex celestial body being projected on a 50-foot screen. Thorne was even able to use the visual rendering to help further develop theories about black holes in the academic sphere.

We ought to point out that, while we'd argue the vast majority of people are impressed by all these visual artifacts of our relationship with space, there remains a contingent who are not. In particular, conspiracy theories abound about how the Earth isn't *really* round, and NASA didn't *really* go to the Moon.

(In another tie-in with film, those who embrace these theories often claim that Stanley Kubrick, who had just completed his sci-fi landmark *2001: A Space Odyssey*, helped stage the Moon landings.) Some of this no doubt comes from the fact that the images are slightly altered—the "Blue Marble" was actually taken "upside-down" relative to how we're used to seeing the Earth on maps—but this is very different from inventing them out of thin air (or, indeed, the vacuum of space). We won't dive into this particular debate except to say, the fact that people have these opinions in the first place says something about the power of ideology—say, the ideology that the Earth is flat or that space is beyond our reach for whatever reason—versus the power of the image. Our discussion of propaganda in Chapter 7 is relevant here, in that some would rather believe that visual evidence is manufactured for nefarious purposes than update their views on the advancement of technology and discovery. But we don't see the fascination with the stars, or the need for their stunning portraits that astronomers provide, going away any time soon. (At least, as sci-fi fans, we hope not.)

Exercises

1. We stressed the hypermediacy of mobility-based games used on smartphones since they are a great example of how the hypermediacy of some visual overlay technologies is very stimulating and fun to work with. But what about a more mundane example? Do you use navigation applications like the ones mentioned in the box above? What kinds of AR occur in those you are familiar with? If it's feasible, try to do a mini-treasure hunt, using handheld navigation to get to an unfamiliar location along an unfamiliar route and compare your experiences to that of others. Take note of your habits when using this form of navigation: how often you have to check the screen, the affordances of the app you're using, etc. How many of the AR functions did

you use and how would you describe them? Is experiencing their hypermediacy the same as what occurs in other AR you are familiar with? Why or why not? (For added perspective, try repeating the exercise *without* looking at your device at all, and see how the feel of it changes.)

2. Do an internet search to look for images of the future; be sure to use specific phrases like "future pavilion," "architecture of the future," or any other combination you think might work. What are some of the ways that visual ideas about the future are part of the images that you find? What is your own emotional reaction to them and how do they make you feel about the future? Create a list of typical "future" ideas in visual culture and consider how they reflect our tendency to think of the future as utopian or dystopian.

3. One of the main problems with both human and algorithmic policing is inherent *bias*. Find a busy location where you can observe a lot of people, and get comfortable. Take *very quick notes* on each person that you can, glancing at them for no longer than five seconds; what do they look like? What kind of a person do you think they are? After you've gotten a good sample—say, a hundred people—*without* looking at the notes, write down what factors you think you paid the most attention to. Did you notice race and ethnicity most often, or presumed gender and orientation? What about height and body shape, clothing, or facial expression?

   Then, type up your text and plug it into a word cloud generator online, or another program that will generate what is called a *rank-frequency plot*, which shows you how often different words come up in the text. (Alternatively, you can count the instances of each descriptor yourself.) What terms and categories did you use most often? Is there a difference between what the data show and the characteristics you thought you noted? If so, why do you think this is?

4. Look online for clips of movies and TV shows set in space from each decade from the 1950s to the present day, whether they are science fiction or some other genre. (A few recommendations are *When Worlds Collide, 2001: A Space Odyssey, The Silent Star/Die schweigende Stern, Star Wars, Star Trek* in any incarnation, *Apollo 13, Gravity*.) What do you notice about the way space is depicted in each case? Look at both the artistic composition (how are planets visually depicted, how is space travel shown, etc.) and the narrative framing (is space beautiful, terrifying, mundane, and so on). There will be some obvious differences between the cases; which are due to the story and/or genre, and why did the creators make those choices? What about differences due to the scientific knowledge that was current at the time and/or the effects technology that was available? Try to imagine what a space travel film will look like 10, 20, and 30 years from now.

For Further Exploration

Hess, Alan. (2004). *Googie redux: Ultramodern Roadside Architecture.* San Francisco, CA: Chronicle Books.

- Hess surveys "Googie," the mid–20th–century architecture style of roadside establishments (especially fast food restaurants) in the United States, and its futurist tendencies.

Sagan, Carl. (1994). *Pale Blue Dot: A Vision of the Human Future in Space.* New York, NY: Ballantine Books.

- A meditation by one of the foremost astronomers of our era, on the Earth and its uniqueness against the vast backdrop of space.

EPILOGUE

We'd like to close this volume with one more exercise that we encourage you to do after finishing this epilogue: put the book down or close your digital reading platform. Get up, put your shoes on, and go outside. Take a short walk to somewhere you go regularly—maybe you have to buy a coffee at the local shop, or pick up some groceries at the supermarket—but take your time to get there. Along the way, see how many things you can find that you had never noticed on your route before, and really pay attention to them. It's okay to focus on the little details, the objects and signs that populate our everyday space, but also try and pause a couple of times to look at the whole scene in front of you. Look at how buildings are arranged on either side of the street; observe the cars going by, and the people you encounter; note the intensity of the sunlight (or streetlights, perhaps) and the clouds in the sky. Then, repeat this exercise, as often as possible.

The immediate point of this book is to give you terminology and concepts to use so that you could talk about ways of seeing in your academic, professional, and maybe even your personal life. But more broadly, our goal has been to get you thinking about how you look at the things around you. It's okay if you're not always sure what the significance is for this or that piece of the visual environment; part of the process of figuring it out is admitting the limitations of your own knowledge. We can't give you a recipe for visual sensitivity, though. It is something you have to develop through practice, and we can only insist that doing so will make you a more thoughtful and considerate person, who is better equipped to perceive *how* and *why* you have the reactions you do to what you see. In the course of writing this book, we have both found ourselves more often keeping our eyes peeled for interesting things that catch our attention, but more importantly, we theorize about what they might mean.

Whether you want to pursue a sweeping program of advertising reform or just be a better video gamer, we hope that you have found the examples, explanations, and discussions in this book useful to your purpose. We encourage you to take a look at some of the readings, documentaries, and other items we have suggested throughout the book, and the references at the end; we wouldn't have included them if they weren't worth looking at. And we urge you to talk with people about their ways of seeing in turn. You don't have to quote passages from these pages— though of course we won't mind—but the simple act of sharing knowledge and perspectives is one of the most powerful things a person can do. As you have opened possibilities for yourself, you can open possibilities for others, helping them make an effort to be more careful interpreters of the visual environment as well.

This book could go on forever, as we live in such a thoroughly visual world; new examples to analyze provide themselves every day. But we will stop here, and leave its continuation in your hands. You are the expert of your own experience, and we trust that you'll know best how to integrate what you've learned here into it. Good luck, and as they say, keep your eyes on the prize ...!

REFERENCES

Barthes, Roland. (1972). *Mythologies*. New York: Hill and Wang.

Bell, Allan. (2008). News stories as narratives. In Jaworski, Adam, & Coupland, Nikolas. *The Discourse Reader*. New York: Routledge. pp. 236–251.

Berlin, Brent, & Kay, Paul. (1991). *Basic Color Terms: Their Universality and Evolution*. Berkeley: The University of California Press.

Bogunjoko, Tayo J., Adekunle O. Hassan, Ogugua Okonkwo, Toyin Akanbi, Mildred Ulaikere, Ayodele Akinye, Halima Bogunjoko, & Monsurat Y. Lawal-Sebioniga. (2018). Impact of middle level eye care personnel on the delivery of eye care services in south-western Nigeria. *International Journal of Community Medicine and Public Health*, 5, 871–879.

Green, Amanda. (2016). "The true story behind this scary meme." Refinery29.com. Accessed August 3, 2020: https://www.refinery29.com/en-us/2016/07/116732/who-is-disaster-girl-meme

Kline, Stephen, Nick Dyer-Witheford, & Grieg de Peuter. (2003). *Digital Play: The Interaction of Technology, Culture, and Marketing*. Montreal & Kingston: McGill-Queen's University Press.

Kuhn, Thomas S. (2012). *The Structure of Scientific Revolutions*. Chicago: University of Chicago Press.

Lago, Federica, Phan Quoc-Tin, & Giulia Boato. (2019). Visual and textual analysis for image trustworthiness assessment within online news. *Security and Communication Networks*. Accessed August 18, 2020: https://doi.org/10.1155/2019/9236910

Lazer, David M. J., Matthew A. Baum, Yochai Benkler, Adam J. Berinsky, Kelly M. Greenhill, Filippo Menczer, Miriam J. Metzger, et al. (2018). The science of fake news. *Science 359*(6380), 1094–1096.

Lenhart, Amanda, Sydney Jones, & Alexandra Macgill. (2008). Adults and video games. Pew Research Center's *Internet and American Life Project*. Accessed August 3, 2020: https://www.pewresearch.org/internet/2008/12/07/adults-and-video-games/

McCloud, Scott. (1993). *Understanding Comics: The Invisible Art*. New York: William Morrow.

Morris, Chris. (2020). Here are the best selling video games of the past 25 years. *Fortune*. Accessed August 3, 2020: https://fortune.com/2020/01/17/best-selling-video-games-past-25-years/

Mulvey, Laura. (1975). Visual pleasure and narrative cinema. *Screen, 16*(3), 6–18.

Nissenbaum, Asaf, & Shifman, Limor. (2018). Meme templates as expressive repertoires in a globalizing world: a cross-linguistic study. *Journal of Computer-Mediated Communication, 23*, 294–310.

Obermaier, Hugo. 1919. *Fossil man in Spain*. New Haven, CT: Yale University Press.

Scollon, Ron, & Scollon, Suzie Wong. (2003). *Discourses in Place: Language in the Material World*. New York: Routledge.

Tufekci, Zeynep. (2017). *Twitter and Tear Gas: The Power and Fragility of Networked Protest*. New Haven, CT: Yale University Press.

Weststar, Joanna, Marie-Josée Legault, Chandell Gosse, & Vicki O'Meara. (2016). *Developer satisfaction survey 2014 & 2015: Diversity in the game industry report*. Accessed August 3, 2020: https://s3-us-east-2.amazonaws.com/igda-website/wp-content/uploads/2019/04/11144431/IGDA_DSS14-15_DiversityReport_Aug2016_Final-1.pdf

Williams, Dmitri, Nicole Martins, Mia Consalvo, & James D. Ivory. (2009). The virtual census: Representation of gender, race, and age in video games. *New media & society, 11*(5), 815–834.

Wolf, Mark J. P. (2001). *The Medium of the Video Game*. Austin, TX: University of Texas Press.

Zittrain, Jonathan L. (2014). Reflections on internet culture. *Journal of Visual Culture, 13*(3), 388–394.

INDEX